The Book of
Bridges

Martin Hayden

GALAHAD BOOKS · NEW YORK CITY

Picture Credits

Edited by Linda Doeser

©Copyright 1976 by Marshall Cavendish Limited

All rights reserved

Library of Congress Catalog Card Number: 76-4054
ISBN 0-88365-358-3

Printed in Great Britain

Published by arrangement with Marshall Cavendish Publications Limited

Designed by Edward Pitcher
Picture research by Sheila A. Thomson

Foreword

BRIDGES REPRESENT THE perfect blending of science and art and the union of function and beauty. No other artefact has so captured the imagination of painters, poets and songwriters and, even today, bridges retain some of the magic and mystery that our forefathers associated with them. Bridges too, reflect the development and decline of civilizations, demonstrating the changing needs of communication, shifts in population, theories of design and advances in technology. *The Book of Bridges* traces their history from simple, functional structures, through the glorious elegance of the Renaissance and the rapid innovation of the Industrial Revolution, to the astounding technological progress of today. Magnificent photographs of the finest examples from Japan to the United States and from Sweden to South Africa illustrate this highly photogenic subject.

No less remarkable than the bridges themselves are the men who designed them. Single mindedly they struggled against vested interests, interference from government departments, insufficient funds, shoddy workmanship, corruption, ignorance and, more than anything, the enormous technical problems of the crossing itself. Many of them destroyed their health and wore themselves out in building the bridges which today stand as monuments to their dedication and imagination.

Contents

Front endpapers *The eleventh century Puenta la Reina in northern Spain.*

Opposite title page *The covered Chapel Bridge over Lake Lucerne in Switzerland.*

Previous page *The Ponte delle Navi at Verona in Italy.*

This page *A canal bridge at Zierikzee in Holland.*

Back endpapers *Pedestrians crossing the Forth Road Bridge in Scotland after the footpaths were first opened.*

Introduction

In October 1931, Franklin D. Roosevelt said *There can be little doubt that in many ways the story of bridge building is the story of civilization. By it, we can readily measure an important part of a people's progress.* He was speaking as the finishing touches were being made to the George Washington Bridge, the main span of which, a clear ¾ mile, was, at the time, double that of any previous bridge. It was a bridge which, despite the Wall Street crash two years earlier, symbolized the United States' technological and financial supremacy in the world. Americans certainly saw it that way.

In no other single type of structure or enterprise, do so many aspects of science, art, technology and social organization come together to produce a single object of which the function is so clear and the form so full of meaning. A historian or an engineer may be able to see detailed and subtle aspects of bridges they study and ordinary people can readily appreciate the strength, size and shape of bridges and the design as well as the

Stringing the suspended truss decking of the Forth Road Bridge in 1963. Building techniques change with each development in transport technology: in the background the Forth Railway Bridge, the greatest bridge of the railway era, can be seen.

labour required to build them.

It is not necessary to be an expert, then, to appreciate bridges as 'signs of the times', because bridges have been built throughout history. A study of bridges can be used as one way of studying history itself. At every stage in the progress of mankind, people have quoted achievements in bridge building as particular examples of general cultural development.

In Roman times, men marvelled at the stone and timber structures providing the dry crossings for the Imperial Armies and the Empire's trade. In the medieval era, the Church and monarchies often bolstered their authority by providing much-appreciated bridges in durable masonry, for farmers, peddlers and pilgrims alike. With the coming of the architect, through the Reformation and the Enlightenment, more delicate bridge designs were admired as expressions of the growing understanding of scientific principles and of the more refined notions of secular beauty. Later, the Industrial Revolution brought many

brutish structures in iron and steel which were considered fantastic, since they were longer and higher than anything which had been possible before. In many nineteenth century bridges we can still see the lack of regard for tradition, and an unstoppable confidence in industry and expansion.

In our own century, many factors have come together to produce the amazing structures of today: the science of materials, the increasing sophistication of design theory, of technology and planning organization, not forgetting the motor car and the acute pressure on urban space. Bridge building will of course continue to develop in the future. As time goes on however, the principle design considerations in bridges (in common with other kinds of buildings or facilities) will change. The main decisions will be concerned less and less with questions like 'Is it technically possible?'. Increasingly, the important questions will be 'Is this socially desirable?' and 'Is building a road and bridge in the situation the best use of limited resources?', or 'Can this crossing be effected with as much safety but at a lower cost?'.

In the history of bridge building, however, the technical developments are crucial and the sheer technical achievements of the bridge builders of the past have to be appreciated clearly. To have this appreciation we must do more than look at the completed structures themselves. We must stand in the shoes of the builder and imagine his view of the crossing before the bridge was begun. This is sometimes a difficult exercise, especially in some locations where the bridge is so much part of the landscape that it is hard to imagine the bridge not there: for example, at places like the Clifton Gorge at Bristol in England, the Firth of Forth in Scotland or the Golden Gate Bay in San Francisco.

Considering the crossing without its bridges and asking ourselves how to begin to build a structure across, we will begin to see the number and complexity of the problems facing the bridge builder. What would be the best principle to use? Which is the most suitable material? Should there be one long span or several short ones? How much would each alternative cost? What sort of foundations are necessary? How will they be dug underwater? What is the best method of erection? Could shipping still use the waterway during construction? How heavy would the bridge need to be to resist wind loading? How light must it be not to fall under its own weight? Will it bend? Will it twist? How much stronger than absolutely necessary need it be for complete safety? And so on and so on.

This book is about how questions like these have been answered at different periods in the development of bridges. It is not however, a text book about engineering. Although the builder and engineer are the most important characters in the bridge building story, bridges are more than the results of construction decisions. The decisions that have been reached have depended on many wider, cultural factors in operation at the time and within the community around the bridge project. When these are taken into account as we stand in the shoes of the engineer contemplating the empty space to be crossed, we can more keenly appreciate the achievements and innovations of the great builders.

Taking an overall view, there are perhaps four main factors which combine to produce a bridge and to determine its style, size and shape. Certainly, the presence of great men of skill and talent is one of these factors. While individual bridge makers of any era have obviously been shaped by the period and environment they lived

Below *Bridge builders of all cultures and ages have embellished their permanent structures to emphasize the importance of them. This cantilever bridge at Wandipore, with its handsome roofed anchor towers is typical of civic structures widespread in China and Tibet.*

Right *Over 600 feet above the Verrazano Narrows, skilled construction workers— 'boomers'—bind the 25,108 steel wires to form the huge cables of the world's biggest suspension bridge.*

Below *Basic structural types: (1) the beam or girder bridge; (2) longer bridges can be achieved by making the beam continuous over intermediate piers; (3) the cantilever—with the ends anchored, projecting beams can form spans with their tips touching, or joined by a light suspended span; (4) the arch, with the downward load of the roadway translated into an outward thrust of the ribs; (5) the suspension bridge, with the roadway slung from cables.*

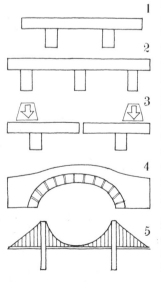

in, certain great men did more than merely apply current wisdom. Without the persistence of Peter of Colechurch, London Bridge would not have been built; without the imagination of Isambard Kingdom Brunel the Royal Albert Bridge would not have been feasible; without the courage of the Roeblings the East River, New York would not have been spanned as early as it was.

The second factor is the general technology of structures and materials and the current practices and working methods in use at any given time. Clearly, there will always be more bridges built employing the well-known techniques than those which employ some revolutionary material or novel construction method. The periods of revolution (as in the change from masonry to iron) and the contributions of the rare innovatory genius (like Thomas Telford) make the most interesting stories. However, the majority of bridges constructed in any period are those which use the 'current wisdom'. The state of the art— the background knowledge—depends to a great extent on the work and experience of previous designers, so that what was revolutionary in one period becomes the accepted practice in the next.

This general level of technology, so important in the final design of a bridge, is not of course a single or a straightforward thing. It consists essentially of two main elements. On one hand, there are ideas about shapes and structural principles and concepts of analyzing stresses; on the other are the materials and their whole range of physical properties, their strengths and weaknesses—their behaviour under various stresses. The relationship between these two elements is not always a direct one. When the first substantial iron bridge was built at Coal-brookdale in Shropshire, although the new material had very different properties from stone, the chosen design was in fact a conservative shape based on the concept of a stone arch. When Robert Stephenson developed the box girder idea for the Britannia Bridge the only material he had to work with was wrought iron. Although his bridge was a landmark in the history of bridge building, the general adoption of the box girder concept was not possible until some 100 years later. By that time, knowledge of steel and concrete had caught up and enabled the box girder principle to be more widely used. In general, the bridges that are judged the most satisfying aesthetically are those in which the design idea and the qualities of the material are most in harmony. The bridges of Robert Maillart are perfect examples.

The third major factor in shaping a bridge is the type of transport for which it is designed. Distinctive types of bridges have evolved for each successive development in transport methods. This is such an obvious point, it needs little elaboration, although, here again, transport methods are closely related to the general level of technology in a given culture, and are themselves among the clearest 'signs of the times'. One only has to compare a primitive footbridge of vines, a stone pack-horse bridge, an iron canal aqueduct, a steel truss railway viaduct and a concrete motorway box girder to appreciate the different requirements of each mode of transport.

The shared characteristic of all the different types of bridge is that they bring people and places closer together. They all facilitate the movement of people, materials and goods by shortening distances and crossing natural barriers to communication. This brings us to the fourth general factor in the creation of bridges—the need to communicate, the need to move about. Generally, this need has been an economic one—the farmer's need to get his produce to market; the nineteenth century coal owner's need to move his product into the townships and industrial areas; the modern manufacturer's need to move raw materials into the factory and the completed goods out to ever wider and more distant markets; the need in developing countries to move natural resources into fast growing local industries or imported foreign goods to the communities that most need them.

This drive towards growth, expansion and ever widening markets has always put the greatest pressure on bridge builders to provide the most direct and economical lines of communication. Bridges then, are useful, functional structures. They bring direct benefits of more straightforward travel and indirect benefits of goods and food-stuffs that, without bridges would be impossible to manufacture or distribute.

The appeal of bridges, however, goes beyond their prosaic functional aspects, beyond their aesthetic appeal; beyond their status as manifestations of civilization. To some people, they appear as perfect symbols of man's creative urge to build, of his need to challenge the natural world by changing it to suit his purpose, of his desire to conquer the void and to bring order out of chaos. These ambitions are of course associated with a certain amount of risk—nature's obstacles are not easily overcome and man has often had to pay dearly for his presumption. From ancient China came stories of the traditions of building live animals into the fabric of bridges by way of sacrifice to the river gods. From medieval Europe many local legends tell of bridge builders facing such difficulties that they sold their souls to the Devil himself for assistance. In all periods to the present day, it has been recognized that 'a bridge demands a life'.

When a bridge fails, it is perhaps these mystical associations that make the disaster so appalling, so much more serious than even the physical calamity of collapse. What failures suggest is that there are, after all, forces and processes that have not been fully understood, that, for all his science, skill and courage, man is not as much in control of himself or his environment as he would like to think.

The imagery of bridges, has long been a favourite in religion and poetry. One of the Pope's

Far left *Six lanes of motor traffic cross between San Francisco and Sausalito beneath the great towers of the Golden Gate Bridge. When it was opened in 1937, the towers were much criticized for their affected architectural style.*

Left *The Tarr Steps, carrying a footpath over the River Barle on Exmoor, date from pre-Christian times. The 17 span clapper bridge appears in the novel* Lorna Doone *as the 'Devil's Bridge'.*

titles is *Pontifex Maximus*—the builder of bridges between God and mankind; William Wordsworth rhapsodized on the view from Westminster Bridge; Henry Longfellow penned a poem on the glories of the Ponte Vecchio. However, perhaps one of the most compelling images comes from the ancient Scandinavian saga *The Younger Edda*, where the bridge is seen in the context of the eternal struggle between good and evil:

Have you not been told that the gods made a bridge from earth to heaven which is called Bifrost. You must have seen it. It may be that you call it the rainbow. It has three colours, it is very strong and is made with more craft and skill than other structures. Still however strong it is, it will break when the sons of Muspel come to ride over it, and then they will have to swim their horses over great rivers to get on ... Bifrost is a good bridge, but there is nothing in the world that is able to stand when the sons of Muspel come to fight.

Here, on the one hand is man's sense of kinship with the gods, symbolized in his appreciation of first bridge making. On the other hand is his anxiety about the power of the untamed elements of destruction, summed up in the image of the sons of Muspel. Bifrost stands, an object of beauty, strength and usefulness, but never quite proof against the unreasoning forces of nature.

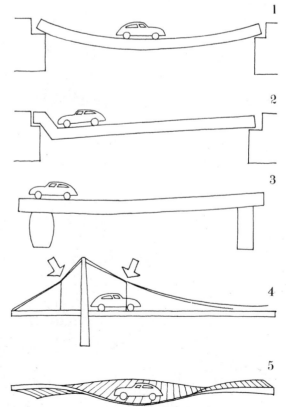

Above *After four hours of swaying and bouncing, 600 feet of the road deck of the Tacoma Narrows Bridge plunged into Puget Sound.*

Left *Stresses in bridge building; the designer must build a structure which will counteract them or must find a shape that will use them to advantage: (1) bending; (2) shear; (3) compression; (4) tension; (5) torsion.*

Above *The timber arch—
Kintaibashi Bridge over the
Nishiki River in Japan.
Originally built in 1673 by
the feudal overlord of the
district, it was exactly
reconstructed in 1953. As
in Europe, traditional ideas
and practical craftsmanship
were usually as important
to the final shape of the
bridge as the truly scientific
analysis of stresses,
materials and economics.*

Centre *The steel arch—
roadway, railway and
footpaths of the Sydney
Harbour Bridge are
suspended from the world's
strongest steel arch. The
decision to choose this
design was influenced by the
inherent visual drama and
vigour of the arch form.*

Below *The concrete arch—
the Paul Sauer Bridge, in
1956, completed the
National Road link
between Cape Town and
Port Elizabeth in South
Africa. One of the world's
foremost designers in
concrete, Riccardo Morandi
of Italy, fully exploited
concrete's economy and
strength in compression to
achieve the 450 foot span
for only £100,000.*

First Bridges

OUR IDEAS ABOUT earliest bridges and how primitive man came to build them, are mostly conjectural. We simply cannot know when the first bridge was built, how it was made or where it happened. This is partly because the history of bridges is the history of ideas as much as the history of the objects themselves. Man may have used a fallen tree over a stream as a bridge years before he thought of chopping one down himself.

Although it is certain that early man lived in groups and passed on his primitive technology to succeeding generations, it is likely that the skill of making a bridge was discovered and rediscovered many times before it became established in any one culture. Apart from coarse stone tools and fossilized bones, the earliest societies have left historians very little to go on, since most of the materials they worked with perished long ago.

To find clues about the first bridges we must look at three things. First, consider the under-populated natural world which stone age man inhabited; second, reconstruct his life style, where he lived, what he ate and so on; third, see what we can learn from the primitive cultures left in the world today.

One popular way of explaining the beginning of bridges is to suggest that man imitated three natural forms to produce the three basic types of bridge. The trunk of a fallen tree across a stream can be seen as a sort of prototype for a beam or girder bridge. Working from nature's model, man needed only to strip off the branches to let each end rest firmly on either bank and to ease passage across the log, and he had made a functional beam bridge. In tropical jungles, the early forest dweller might have observed vines and creepers growing between trees across streams, and have used them to clamber up and swing over the gap. What he had to do was to find similar plants of the right type, length and strength, tie them firmly at each end, high enough for the sag to clear the water's surface, and he had produced a suspension bridge. The third natural phenomenon to suggest a bridge-form could have been a fall of rocks, jamming against each other in such a way as to form an accidental arch. Alternatively, an arch may have been suggested by natural rock arches carved out by water or wind. However, the leap in imagination and the skill required actually to make an arch, would have been far beyond the earliest constructors.

This idea of early man adapting examples from nature is really more use in understanding bridge principles than an actual account of what happened. For the thousands of years of the Paleolithic era, up to about 8000 BC, the main pattern of living was a wandering, hunting and gathering existence. All members of the tribes would follow the herds of deer or buffalo as they searched for pasture in the changing seasons. Their hunting techniques and indeed the mystic life associated with them, were complex and profound, to judge by cave paintings like those at Lascaux and Altamira. However, the need for permanent routes, like the need for permanent homes, was not enough to stimulate the construction of bridges.

Very slowly, man began to control his surroundings. The hunter realized that he could take a hand in the feeding and the breeding of useful animals; the craftsman refined and specialized his production of tools and discovered the skills of potting and weaving; the food gatherer learned enough about habitat and growth of plants to grow them himself. All these, combined with a dawning awareness of metals, completed the Neolithic revolution. For at least part of the year settlements about the tribal fields and animal pens became more permanent. Most likely there were more dealings with other groups—stock to be stolen or a grain surplus to be bartered. So regular routes between settlements became necessary. At this stage of development, the question 'Why go all the way round when you could go straight across?' begins to have some meaning.

Neolithic cultures

Spreading outwards from the fertile crescent area of north Africa and the Middle East, and quite probably from pockets in India and China, more aggressive attitudes towards the environment were reflected in many different materials and forms of bridge building. In wooded areas, the polished stone axe was developed and used for cutting and trimming logs for simple beam bridges. Laying two logs parallel, first together, then separated and the gap floored with cross pieces, would have improved the carrying capacity and convenience of the structures. In thinly forested areas, the beam could be fashioned from a slab of rock. The remains of monuments like Stonehenge and New Grange burial chamber demonstrate, not only the skill and scale of workmanship possible with stone, but also the awareness of an important principle: that, not only was it possible to erect a beam on which to cross a space, but also the supports for the beam could be made.

In jungles and mountainous forests, the techniques of plaiting and weaving brought development in the primitive suspension bridge. Woven floors could be strung between two plaited vines and other refinements, like handrails, could be added.

There are other fundamental advances dating from Neolithic times. Once the idea of building a support at each end was established, it became possible to build a multi-span bridge. This principle made it feasible to erect structures over wider obstacles by setting up a number of supports of single rocks or piles of stones, and simply joining them with slabs of stone or timber beams. Postbridge on Dartmoor in England is an example. Although its actual date has not been established exactly (it is possibly thirteenth century), its design is definitely prehistoric. Three 15 foot granite slabs rest on four piers of granite blocks, and the sheer weight of the structure is

Right Natural accidents could have suggested basic bridge making ideas to primitive man: (1) fallen tree—the beam bridge; (2) vines and creeping plants— the suspension bridge; (3) fallen rocks—the arch.

Previous page The 'Clam bridge' is one of the most primitive bridge types. The Teign-e-ver bridge spans the Walla Brook on Dartmoor, England, with a single granite slab.

Above far right In wooded areas, logs could be cut by the earliest Neolithic communities, to form a simple beam bridge. In this traditional Japanese example, a central timber pier adds to the stiffness.

Below right A primitive bridge over the Spiti River in the Himalayas. Log spans can be made more convenient by the addition of a floor of rough planks. The overall span can be increased by resting the beam on a primitive cantilever of projecting logs weighted down by the piers.

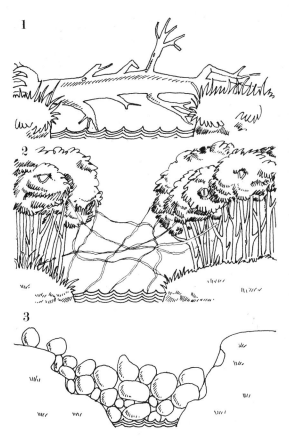

enough to preserve it from the periodic flooding of the East Dart River. Britain has several examples of this type of bridge, including the famous 'Tarr Steps' over the River Barle on Exmoor, which appears as the Devil's Bridge in *Lorna Doone*. The British examples, however, pale before the fabulous thirteenth century Lo Yang bridge in the Fu kien province of China, with stone slabs with a clear 70 foot span.

The earliest written record of a multi-span bridge appears in the works of Herodotus, the Greek historian who lived in the fifth century BC. He describes a bridge across the River Euphrates, linking the royal palaces of ancient Babylon on each bank. A hundred stone piers supported wooden beams of cedar, cypress and palm, to form a structure no less than 35 feet wide and 660 feet long. He also mentions that the flooring between the beams could be removed at night as a precaution against invaders.

According to legend, earlier in Babylon there had been a single huge brick arch of 660 feet on this site, erected by order of Nimrod, third ruler after Noah. Although the arch had been developed for buildings in Mesopotamia in the third and fourth centuries BC, a brick arch of this scale would have been technologically impossible.

How exactly the arch came to be invented is again a matter for conjecture. Both the Sumerian and Egyptian cultures have provided examples of

The date of Postbridge over the East Dart River on Dartmoor is not known exactly, but the concept is a primitive one. With such 'Clapper' bridges, wider streams could be crossed by using several slabs of granite resting on piers of rough-hewn stone. The sheer weight of stone in this multi-span structure secures it against flood damage.

arched windows and vaults. The oldest example found so far, is in Egypt at Dindereh, dating from about 3600 BC, and there are several specimens in Mesopotamia from a century or so later. Such 'voussoir' arches, constructed from a row of wedge-shaped stones or bricks, represent a great development from the first type of arch to be constructed, the corbelled or false arch. Each course of stones or bricks either side of an opening was laid projecting slightly further than the one below, until the two sides met at the crown.

It took centuries, however, before the idea of supporting the weight of a structure by changing the vertical force of gravity into a sideways thrust, was applied on any scale in bridge building. Beginning with the Romans, the stone arch was to become Europe's principle technique of bridging for almost 1800 years. The invention of the arch, then, was a very significant step. As David Steinman, the American bridge designer, said in his book *Bridges and their Builders:*
The arch principle is an essential; it is a vital element in almost all kinds of building. Its introduction brought forth a new impulse, an organic or dynamic building force, which was expressed by the form itself. The post and lintel type of construction, on the other hand, is static, inorganic, it does not transmit a feeling of movement and power, only of inert mass.

There is evidence that other structural

principles were discovered or invented a very long time before they reached important expression in bridge building. Examples may be found in the archaeological remains of the 'lake dwellers' of Switzerland, early Bronze Age communities of about 2500 BC, who lived in small timber houses built on platforms over a lake. The supports for these platforms were provided by timber piles driven vertically into the lake bed. The craft of driving timber piles was important, not only because it predicted the evolution of timber trestle bridges, but also because it suggested a method of providing relatively firm foundations for heavy structures on a soft surface. Further, the roof members of the lake dwellers' houses consisted of beams with their bottom ends resting on the end of the horizontal lintel, and their top ends leaning together. Although in a very simple form, the basis of the truss was thus established. This is based on the geometric principle that a triangle is the only shape which cannot be changed without altering the length of any of its sides.

Another principle which evolved before proper historical records were kept, was a further use of the versatile beam. By anchoring one end of the beam very firmly at the bank, and by supporting it on a pier close to its fixed end, a beam could be made to project some distance unsupported, like a springboard. This is the cantilever. Two such structures could be built face to face with the tips of the projecting arms either touching, or close enough to be bridged by a light suspended span. Bridges on the cantilever principle are still erected in the Hindu Kush region of Afghanistan, using rough timbers and stones from the river bed.

Suspension spans

The most notable achievements of early cultures, mostly with a non-metal technology, are the so-called 'primitive' suspension bridges. To this day in South America, Africa and south-east Asia, bridges are constructed for daily use from vines, creepers and bamboo. European travellers in these regions in the eighteenth and nineteenth centuries never failed to comment on the apparent shakiness of these structures, but for the local communities not encumbered by masses of baggage, they were clearly satisfactory. A typical report comes from a certain Captain Gerard. Exploring in the Himalayas in the early nineteenth century, he describes a 'suzum'—five or six wicker twig cables twisted together to walk on, with a pair of lighter cables for handrails, linked to the main cable every two feet or so.
Frequent accidents have occurred, and, only a month before I crossed in August last, two people were lost by one of the side ropes giving way. The guides that accompanied me did not tell me of this until they saw ten or twelve of my followers on the bridge at once . . . . The news of the late accident spread rapidly; some of my people were so alarmed they could move neither one way or the other and stood trembling for a long time. Two in greater

terror than the rest, precipitated my tent into the Sutledge.

This bridge appears to have been a hammock or tubular type of suspension span where the footway and handrails are all woven together. In some parts of South America this type of bridge is called the 'Bejuco' bridge, after the fibrous plant used in weaving the cables. There is a great variety in types of primitive suspension bridge. Some consist of a roadway of bamboo or planks laid directly on to the structural cables. There were reports of 150 foot spans over the Apimurac River in the Andean gorges of Peru. In India and China various contraptions were discovered, baskets, loops or forked sticks, for sliding along single cables stretched over ravines. One type which predicted the principle of the modern suspension bridge was found in Nepal. Lengths of plaited grass cable were fastened at the banks, and, although they sagged considerably in the centre, the roadway was nearly level since it was suspended from the main ropes by lighter vertical cables.

The suspension bridges highlight the common features of all primitive bridges—they were used by small numbers of people who mostly would have travelled on foot for domestic, local purposes. They would have been made from easily available materials. What these available materials were, what the nature of the obstacle was, and what local custom and experience suggested, were all factors in deciding what form the bridge would take. Even to the small communities of the time, however, a bridge would have offered a way of crossing natural obstacles distinctly preferable to fording, swimming or making long, exhausting detours.

As man evolved his technologies beyond stone, timber and brick to include small quantities of copper, bronze and even iron, he also improved his social organization and his farming techniques. So man was able to live in larger communities. Consequently, roads and bridges became more and more important for the movement of men and goods for conquest and trade. European and Near Eastern history was marked by the rise and fall of several great civilizations—Persian, Greek and Roman—each of which left its mark on bridge building in varying degrees.

China

China, however, was a world of its own. Its traditions of bridge building were very ancient, going back to the reign of Emperor Yao around 2300 BC. The Chinese built a variety of bridge types—simple beam, cantilever, suspension— which changed very little for centuries. The methods of construction were all characterized by strict ideas of economy, suitability for the site and the purpose of the bridge. For example, a small rural bridge over a shallow stream needed only a timber beam structure supported on piers made of bamboo baskets filled with rubble. An estuary or wider river would have required one, or

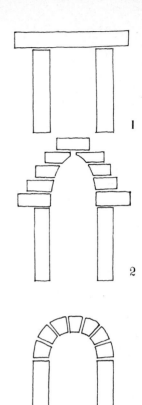

Above *The different solutions to the problem of bridging an opening were probably first evolved for buildings: (1) post and lintel; (2) the corbelled arch; (3) the voussoir arch.*

perhaps more, suspension spans, with cables of split bamboo, skillfully twisted together and slung between capstans in the bridge houses at each end. The bridge in the village or town centre would have been a grander cantilever. These were originally built with wooden towers at each end, filled with rubble or stone, in which the projecting cantilever arms were anchored. As stone cutting improved, between 400 and 300 BC, stone towers appeared. The bridge in the centre of the community would have been the place for folk to meet, gossip and do business.

Persia and Greece

The Chinese had also used pontoon bridges very early on, linking rows of sampans, anchored parallel to the stream, with rows of planks. In Europe and the Near East, in the surviving histories of early civilizations, pontoon bridges played a decisive part. Although not the first, the most celebrated was that thrown across the Dardanelles by the Persian ruler Xerxes in his efforts to keep the rising power of the Greeks at bay, in the fifth century BC. Herodotus provides the record. As the bridge was being built, a storm wrecked the partially built structure. In his fury, Xerxes ordered the engineer to be beheaded, the sea to be given 300 lashes and a pair of manacles to be cast into the water to make the spirits of the sea behave. The replacement engineer was more successful. Six hundred and seventy-four boats—triremes and penteconters—were anchored in two rows. Six cables—four of papyrus and two of flax

—were stretched along each row, and sawn logs were laid across the cables to form the floor. The floor was completed with stamped earth and brushwood and bulwarks were erected to screen the animals from the sight of the sea. Herodotus claims it took seven days and seven nights for the two million strong Persian army to cross the bridge into Greece. Although this huge force crushed the Greek land armies, the subsequent Greek naval victory at Salamis forced the Persians to retreat homewards across the bridge.

Little is known of other types of Persian bridges at this time. A 20-span bridge of brick arches over the Diz in Khuzistan province may date from the third century BC. It is thought that the Chinese forces guarding silk caravans first encountered arches in Parthia, the inheritor of the Persian Empire, and took the idea back with them in the first century AD. The earliest Chinese arches began to appear after that date, a rare example of a foreign idea being incorporated into the established Chinese culture.

The Greeks, for all the achievements in social ideas, philosophy, drama, mathematics and architecture, did not contribute a great deal to the development of bridges. The main lines of communication between the city states were by sea rather than over land. While the arch was certainly known by the fifth century BC, the preferred style of building was based on the post and lintel. Assos in Lydia is the site of a typical Greek beam bridge—17 stone piers, ten feet apart, support two foot-wide stone beams. Other examples can still be found in the early Greek

Below left In China and Tibet, the design of cantilever bridges changed little over some 3000 years. Stone towers anchor the cantilever timbers, and the roadway, complete with railings and roof, was often used by villagers as a place for gossip or business.

Below right Not all 'primitive' suspension bridges are narrow and precarious. In this example from North Burma, the fine cane floor is suspended from fibre rope and is designed for mule transport.

provinces of Sparta, Mycena and Messenia. Apart from one or two fine Greek arches like the 27 foot bridge at Pergamon, it was left to the Romans to develop it most fully as a bridging technique.

The Romans

The Romans were masters of all practical skills. They evolved superior techniques in iron smelting, tool making, building, surveying and warfare, which enabled them to colonize virtually all the known world of Europe and the Mediterranean. From Rome the legions gradually spread a way of life—language, social organization and technology—to thousands of local tribes and communities. Plunder and slaves from the conquered peoples, precious metals for the imperial mint, spices and exotic foods for the city dwellers' tables were sent back to Rome. The Romans understood that the establishment and maintenance of their empire depended upon efficient and permanent communications. Building roads and bridges was therefore high priority.

In their building, the Romans used all kinds of materials with great expertise. Wood was treated with alum for fire-proofing and oils and resin for rot-proofing. Stone was carefully chosen; the yellowish Tufa was widely used but had to be weatherproofed with a stucco finish; Travertine, harder and greyer, would withstand weather but would lose its compressive strength in fire. Bricks of white clay, red earth and sand would be left two years to dry. The Romans' biggest breakthrough was the discovery and exploitation of a natural cement, based on a volcanic clay called pozzuolana. They occasionally used it as mortar for laying bricks or stones and also developed the first concrete, by mixing it with burnt lime, sand and stone chips. A sixth century bridge at Amalfi in this material is still standing.

However, the first Roman bridges were of wood. The most ancient was the Pons Sublicius, or Bridge of Piles, over the River Tiber. The original bridge was built in 621 BC and was the one featured in Macaulay's *How Horatio Kept the Bridge* in *Lays of Ancient Rome*. The most interesting thing about the bridge is its association with Roman religious life. It is thought that the priests of the *Collegium Pontifices* built the bridge. The head of this institution was called *Pontifex Maximus*, which means greatest maker of bridges. The title was later taken over by Roman emperors and later still by the Pope. This demonstrates just how important, even sacred, the idea of bridge building was in men's minds. The practices of the *Collegium* priests were originally derived from the *terramare* communities of the north Italian lakes, local variants of the lake dwellers further north.

The Pons Sublicius was also the site of an annual Roman ritual. On the Ides of May a procession of virgins and praetors cast effigies of old men into the Tiber. This ancient ritual was probably itself a relic of an even earlier practice

In mountainous regions, like parts of Korea, early explorers had to make use of vegetable suspension bridges erected by local people. Overloading and sheer fright caused frequent accidents although more often such structures saved many miles of backbreaking detour.

of human sacrifice. The irate gods of the river must be appeased lest they throw too many difficulties in the path of the imprudent humans attempting to erect a structure across it.

As the Romans began their expansion, the first step was usually military conquest. Like Xerxes, Caesar often used pontoon bridges for his armies' movements. Caesar, however, also used a temporary trestle structure, which he described in some detail in his *Commentaries*, a diary of his conquests. In 55 BC his invading legions crossed

the Rhine on a timber trestle structure about 1400 feet long, 40 feet wide, with beams 25 feet long, supported on piles driven into the river bed. The upstream piles were driven slanting against the current and were each protected by three vertical piles to form a cutwater. Caesar boasted that the bridge took only ten days to put up after all the timber had been assembled.

However, the Romans used stone for permanent bridges and several examples of the characteristic semi-circular arches of finely cut voussoirs can

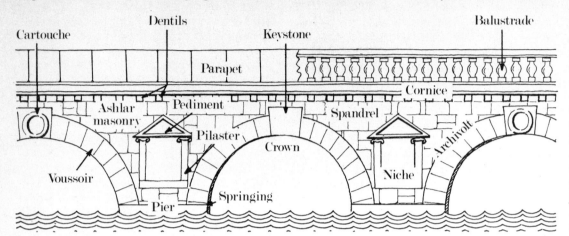

Left Some architectural terms used in Roman and later masonry arches.

Below The Ponte di Augusto over the River Marecchia at Rimini. It was completed in 20 AD and is the best preserved of the Roman stone bridges in Italy. Its classic proportions and fine decorations provided the original model for many designs of Palladian architects from the sixteenth century on.

Left *The Roman Empire reached its greatest extent in the time of the Emperor Trajan. The pictorial record of his conquest of Dacia (roughly equivalent to present day Hungary), on Trajan's Column in Rome depicts the legions' crucial crossing of the Danube on pontoon and trestle bridges.*

magnificent unadorned six-span bridge, 650 feet long. It was built by Caius Julius Lacer on the order of the Emperor Trajan in 105 AD. Although refurbished from time to time, it probably looks much the same now as it did in Roman times, with its two 100-foot central spans 200 feet above the river. Alcantara also demonstrates a particular feature of Roman bridge building in that it has triangular cutwaters on the upstream side of each pier, to reduce the wearing effect of the flowing river.

The other great demonstrations of Roman bridge building skills are to be seen in several aqueducts still standing. The most extended and complex water supply scheme was that built for Rome itself, but the two most remarkable aqueducts are in France and Spain. The two tiers of 109 arches in total of the Segovia Aqueduct carried the waters of the River Frío the last 2500 feet into the town. Originally constructed at the end of the first century AD, it was partially broken down by the Moors in the religious wars of the fifteenth century. In 1483, Queen Isabella commissioned a monk to rebuild it to its original pattern. Although the repairs were good for three centuries, when the aqueduct was again refurbished in the eighteenth century, the Roman stonework needed little attention.

The most famous of the Roman aqueducts is the Pont du Gard near Nîmes, in what was then Transalpine Gaul. Three tiers of arches march across the valley 150 feet above the River Gard; six on the lower tier, with spans between 53 and 80 feet, 11 in the middle row the same size and 36 on the top row, with spans of 15 feet 9 inches. This huge structure, nearly 900 feet long, was built mostly of dry stone—only the top tier of small arches has its stones laid in mortar. The aqueduct is said to have been built on the orders of Agrippa, son-in-law of Augustus, in about 19 BC and it has amazed travellers ever since. The philosopher Jean-Jacques Rousseau described his reactions in the eighteenth century.

I walked along the three stages of this superb construction with a respect that almost made me shrink from treading on it. The echo of my footsteps under the immense arches made me think I could hear the strong voices of the men who had built it. I felt lost like an insect in the immensity of the work. I felt, along with the sense of my own littleness, something which nevertheless seemed to elevate my soul. I said to myself with a sigh, 'Oh that I had been born a Roman.'

Rousseau, however, might not have been so keen on the idea of being a Roman slave. For although the Roman masters knew well the skills of cutting and laying stones, driving piles and erecting scaffolding, such work could not have been completed without a huge amount of backbreaking work by slave labour.

Nevertheless, the achievements of the empire were enormous. When it could no longer sustain itself and eventually collapsed, nothing like the Roman roads, buildings or bridges was seen in Europe again for centuries.

Above The highest section of the Roman aqueduct at Segovia in Spain. Many large structures like this were linked to provide Rome's own lavish water supply, but none of the Italian examples is so well preserved. A medieval legend tells how the Devil, seeking the favours of a young maid, built the bridge one night to ease her chore of water carrying.

Right The three tiers of the Pont du Gard in Southern France, constructed around the second decade AD. The most stupendous of the Roman aqueducts, it was one link in a 25-mile system to bring water to Nîmes. The projecting blocks in the middle tier were built in to support wooden scaffolding and the falsework for the voussoir stones of the arches.

still be seen in Rome and in the Romanized provinces. Rome itself contained eight masonry bridges. Six remain, although they have undergone major repairs, rebuilding and alteration over the centuries since they were built. In order of erection they are Ponte Rotto (179 BC), Ponte Molle (110 BC), Ponte Quattro Capi (62 BC), Ponte Cestius (45 BC), Ponte Sant'Angelo (136 AD) and Ponte Sisto (370 AD). The Pons Sublicius disappeared finally in 1877 and the present Ponte Sublicio on the same site is made of iron. The builders of these bridges in the capital lavished, not only great care and skill in cutting and dressing the voussoir stones, but also great artistry in their decoration. Both the Ponte Rotto and the Ponte Sant'Angelo are heavily decorated, but Roman bridge decoration is best seen in the Pons Augustus at Rimini. The line of the roadway is accentuated by a cornice; the piers are adorned with pilastered niches and the arch keystones carry cartouches.

Outside Rome itself, in general, there was not so much emphasis on the monumental or decorative additions to the bridges—they were built to do a job. Europe was traversed by a network of Roman roads and it was said that, having crossed the English Channel, a Roman Briton could travel to the capital itself without once fording a stream. While this is probably a wild claim, it does imply that there were hundreds of large and small Roman arches on the continent. The bridges which remain tend to be the grandest and most spectacular examples. At Alcantara in Spain, the Roman road crossed the River Tagus on a

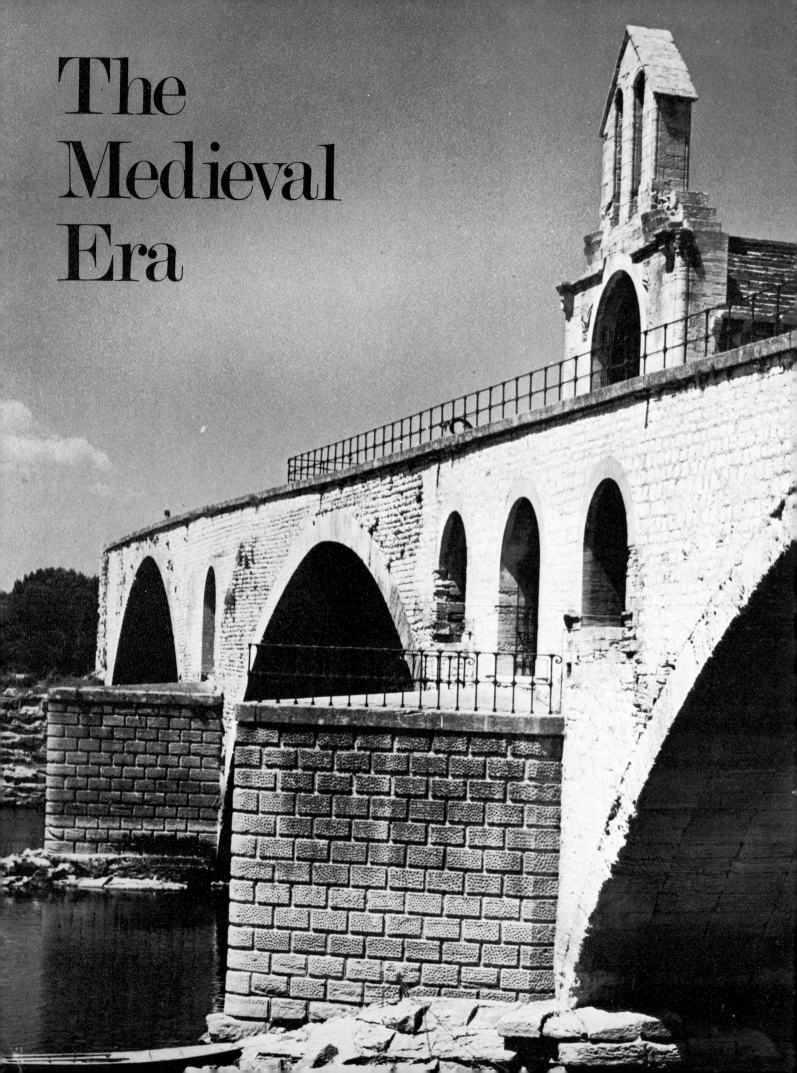

The
Medieval
Era

DESPITE THEIR SKILL in building roads and bridges, their ability to colonize and organize established farming and marketing communities, and the renown of their armies, the Romans could not protect their empire from local tribes and peoples at its margins. Gradually, more and more troops were recalled to Rome and the colonized communities were left to fend for themselves. As the Huns, Saxons and Danes took over the Romanized areas, northern Europe fell into the 'Dark Ages'. As the organization of the empire collapsed, the technological skills it was based upon disappeared. For example, concrete was not to be used again until its rediscovery at the end of the eighteenth century.

Further, with the empire fragmented into smaller tribal types of communities who were more or less continually at war with each other, there was no longer the need for long-range overland travel. Bridge building in the Dark Ages was therefore not significant, as far as we can tell, for there are very few written records from the sixth to the tenth centuries. Work on bridges tended to be concentrated upon either the maintenance of existing Roman structures, or the building of basic timber trestles.

However, in its last stages, the Roman Empire was a Christian empire. Although nearly every other aspect of Roman culture was to disappear, small groups of monks sealed themselves off from the barbaric life around them to live a life of work, study and prayer in half-forgotten monasteries. The next great impetus for civilization came from these churchmen, who had preserved and developed both spiritual and practical knowledge. The spread of faith into the community at large, and the establishment of the Church's authority were more or less complete in Europe by about 1000 AD.

The medieval era got under way with something of a building boom in roads and bridges as well as churches, monasteries and cathedrals. Travel became more wide ranging again, especially with the Crusades to the Holy Land. Europeans were confronted with the brilliance and vigour of Islamic art and building and brought the idea of the Gothic arch home with them.

The Brothers of the Bridge

Bridge building became one of several activities in which certain religious orders specialized. In northern Italy lived a group of friars of the Altopascio order at the Hospice of St James, near Lucca. These monks were skilled in carpentry and building as well as in the care and protection of pilgrims and travellers. After the construction of their earliest bridge over the White Arno, the fame of the *Fratres Pontifices* (Brothers of the Bridge) spread to France, where a group of Benedictine monks started a similar group. The most famous of the French *Frères Pontiffes* was the Order of Saint Jacques du Hauts Pas, whose great hospice in Paris stood on the site of the

present church of that name. Their activities included building bridges, maintaining ferries and providing hostels for pilgrims and travellers. With their red cross and bridge design emblazoned on their white habits, the brothers were deeply appreciated and revered throughout France. The Pont Saint-Esprit over the River Rhône was built by these Frères Pontiffes, but more famous by far, is the neighbouring bridge at Avignon.

Legend has it that a shepherd lad named Bénézet interrupted mass one day with an announcement that he had been sent by God to build a bridge across the Rhône. He is reported to have proved his divine backing to the incredulous bishop by miraculously shifting a huge boulder at the site where, he maintained, the bridge was to be built. It is not clear what relationship existed between Bénézet and the order of Saint Jacques du Haut Pas, but between 1177 and 1187, with the active support of the Church, he planned and organized the building of this large and beautiful structure. He was held in such reverence for this great work that on his death he was canonized and buried in the bridge's little chapel.

The bridge originally consisted of more than 20 arches, two sets of spans over water and a third

Previous page Three of the remaining spans of the Pont d'Avignon, the world's most famous chapel bridge. When it was built in the twelfth century it consisted of more than 20 arches across the River Rhône. Its builder, Bénézet, was canonized for his great work and was buried in the little chapel on the bridge.

set, of perhaps half a dozen arches, over the Isle de Barthelasse in the middle of the river. The original version of the famous song of the bridge ran, *Sous le pont d'Avignon* (under Avignon bridge), and it is thought that it was beneath these central arches that the dance took place. It has never been established exactly how many arches the bridge had—sadly, only four spans now remain, varying between 101 and 110 feet.

The chapel on the bridge reflects the piety and philanthropic purpose of its builders and many medieval structures share this feature. However, the narrowing of the roadway, from 16 to 6 feet, on the Pont d'Avignon highlights another quite different function which many bridges of the time had to perform—that of defence. In the continuing feudal disputes of the period, bridges were obviously useful as crossing places, and consequently were key tactical and defensive positions.

In England, the monks of the Brotherhood of the Bridge were not as active in bridge construction as their French counterparts, since lay organizations, like the trades and crafts guilds, had grown up. Even so, many medieval bridges in Britain were built by local abbeys and religious houses, begun on Church funds and maintained by

Above *Medieval bridges financed and built by the Church often featured a chantry—a shelter for travellers to offer both prayers and alms for the bridge's maintenance. This bridge at Bradford on Avon, England was built in the 1300s, although the chapel's domed roof dates from the seventeenth century when it was re-built.*

Left *A minor emblem of the Church's role in medieval bridge construction—a cross socket in the parapet of Radcot Bridge over the River Thames.*

offerings and alms collected from small chapels built into the bridge. None of these 'chapel bridges' remains as it was built. In addition to the wear of centuries, the anti-Catholic fervour of King Henry VIII's and Oliver Cromwell's times resulted in many being destroyed or modified and put to other uses.

One of the earliest chapel bridges was Elvet Bridge in Durham, built with a chapel at each end in 1174, under the aegis of Hugh Pudsey, Bishop of Durham. Mostly, however, chapel bridges incorporated a single building which may have been anything between a shelter for offering passing prayers, and a fully functioning church, with a full-time priest and regular services. An example of the first type is the stone bridge at Bradford-on-Avon, in Wiltshire. Originally built in the fourteenth century, it still has a small 'chapel for Mass', or oratory, built on one of the river piers. Originally the bridge was little more than a pack-horse and foot bridge, but in the seventeenth century it was widened, and the oratory was given a domed, stone roof. At the other end of the scale is Wakefield Bridge with its large chapel of St Mary. In 1358, the priests, William Kaye and William Bull, had £10 a year settled on them by Edward III 'for ever to perform Divine service in a chapel of St Mary newly built on the bridge at Wakefield'. The 'forever', of course, was too optimistic and the chapel was used as a warehouse after the dissolution and suffered major rebuilding by Sir Gilbert Scott in the nineteenth century. The only other surviving chapel bridges in England are over the Ouse at St Ives in Huntingdonshire

and at Rotherham in Yorkshire.

Not every medieval bridge boasted an actual chapel, but many of them carried more minor emblems of their religious associations. Many of them had a cross mounted either at the ends or over the central span. The crosses have long since disappeared but the fourteenth century Radcot Bridge over the Thames has an interesting stone detail over the central span, which was probably a cross socket.

Secular constructions

Although the church was the institution which dominated most aspects of spiritual and temporal life, it did not maintain a monopoly in bridge building, especially in Britain. As the trade guilds grew, landowners, barons and even organized local communities began to commission the master masons and carpenters to construct bridges. In Europe the order of the Frères Pontiffes was eventually suppressed in 1459 by Pope Pius II.

Examples of guild commissioned bridges can be found in the building of Abingdon and Culham bridges over the Thames from 1446. They were sponsored and organized by the Guild of the Holy Cross—an organization of wealthy and charitable townsfolk, mostly wool merchants. Each contributed what he could in money, rents from properties and stone from his own quarries. The whole town took on the responsibility of maintaining the bridges once they were built. The reasons for the enterprise were charitable and the Guildsmen were anxious to carry out 'good works'

Above Part of the refurbished Abingdon Bridge over the River Thames. The original bridge was started in 1446, not by the Church, but by a guild of charitable and wealthy tradesmen of the town.

Right *The fortified Monmow Bridge at Monmouth. Built in the thirteenth century, the original bridge was the width of the gateway. The extra ribs to support footpaths had to be added later when wheeled traffic created dangerous bottlenecks.*

Below *The Pont Valentré at Cahors in France. With its three defensive towers, it was completed in 1355 after nearly 50 years of building.*

of benefit to all. There is no doubt, however, that the bridges increased the fortunes of Abingdon and its inhabitants by enabling the town to take over from Wallingford as the best embarkation point for river traffic to London.

Fortified bridges

A very distinctive medieval type of bridge was the fortified bridge at key river crossings, frequently in border country. In the developing nations of Europe, the power of the kings was continuously being challenged, often by rival groups of ambitious noblemen, and so wars and battles for supremacy were frequent. Movement about the country was always a key factor for the private armies of medieval barons and warlords, and river crossings were of great tactical importance. Further, the great towns of medieval England, like Durham, York and Chester, were often built on defensible sites on rivers and the bridge into the settlement was frequently fortified for the protection of the whole town. Thus records show that there were fortified bridges once in all three cities. Fortifications often took the form of a narrow gateway through a tower built across the bridge. When wheeled vehicles began to become more regular in the eighteenth century, these old defences often created a serious obstruction to traffic movement, so they have since been removed.

The two remaining fortified bridges in Britain are at Monmouth in Wales and Warkworth in Northumberland. Stirling Bridge was another key point. For years the lowest bridge-point over the Forth, it carried the only route to the north of Scotland until the eighteenth century. The present bridge, dating from around 1400, is no longer fortified. Its predecessor was the scene of the Battle of Stirling in 1297. An English army led by the Earl of Surrey was marching northwards against the rebellious Scottish forces of Sir William Wallace. Stirling Bridge was so narrow that the English troops could not cross more than two abreast. Wallace waited until half the army had crossed and then descended on the bridge head. The English force, cut in two, could neither advance nor retreat, and the majority of the English who had already crossed were speared or drowned. Eight years later, Wallace's head was the first of many to be exhibited on Old London Bridge.

Devil's bridges

One splendid example of the medieval fortified bridge can be seen at Cahors in France. The Pont Valentré was built on the initiative of the townspeople, who raised a special tax on any merchandise which came through the city gates to pay for its building. The bridge took nearly 50 years to build, between 1308 and 1355. Although the local bishop, Raymond Panchielli, was mainly responsible for organizing the building, there is a local legend that this is a 'Devil's Bridge'.

The builder in charge of construction, worried with slow progress, accepted the devil's offer of help in exchange for his soul. Part of the bargain was that Satan was to do exactly as the builder directed. As the bridge reached completion, the builder saved his soul by ordering the devil to carry water in a sieve. Furious at being tricked, the devil frustrated attempts to complete the bridge by continually removing one particular stone in the central tower as soon as it was set in place. The stone is missing to this day.

The idea of 'Devil's Bridges' was particularly strong in medieval times and the legends take many different forms. When the Brotherhood of the Bridge was at the height of its influence, it was said that any bridge not built by the monks was a 'Devil's Bridge'.

Another story comes from Wales. The River Mynach, near Aberystwyth, is nowadays spanned by three bridges, built at different times, one above the other. The lowest and oldest Pont-y-Mynach, was probably built by the Knights Hospitallers, but a local poem describes how the devil, disguised as a monk, threw it up to help an old lady and her dog over the ravine. The one condition was that she should give him the first living thing to cross. As she was invited to try the bridge, she spotted a cloven hoof beneath the robe, so:
In her pocket she fumbled, a crust out tumbled,
She called her little black cur:
The crust over she threw, the dog after it flew
Says she, 'The dog's yours, crafty sir!'
The devil always comes off worst. Similar stories are told about 'Devil's Bridges' like the Pont de Diable in the St Gothard Pass, Switzerland, the bridge at Kirkby Lonsdale in Westmorland England, and one of the bridges over the Main at Frankfurt.

Upkeep and maintenance

Whatever the origins of medieval bridges, their upkeep was always a problem to the individual or the community responsible. There were so few bridges that those which did exist were used very

Right High Bridge in Lincoln. The houses erected on some medieval and Tudor bridges provided rents for the upkeep of the arch and roadway. They were also relatively healthy places to live.

Below left Local legend surrounds the oldest of the three spans of the Pont-y-Mynach in Wales. The Devil is said to have put up the bridge in an instant but, as in most stories of this kind, his efforts failed to win any souls.

Below right Ribbed arches, double-sided cutwaters and narrow roadways characterize many medieval bridges. The Devil's Bridge at Kirkby Lonsdale in Westmorland dates from the thirteenth century and carries an 11 foot roadway 180 feet over the River Lune.

heavily. What written records of medieval bridges remain, are often about the costs and problems of maintenance and repair.

One way of raising money was to build houses and shops on the bridge, and to use the rents to finance repairs. Old London Bridge was the most spectacular example of this, but there were several other housed bridges like Lincoln High Bridge and the Ponte Vecchio in Florence. Alternatively, bridges could be maintained on the proceeds of tolls collected. 'Pontage', or the right to collect tolls, could only be granted by the king and was commonly granted for a few years at a time. For example, the Patent Rolls of 1252, during the reign of Henry III, describe how pontage was first granted to:

The bailiff and good men of Fordingbrig for the remaking and repair of the bridge which the king hears is in a ruinous state.

The toll, one halfpenny per cart and one farthing per horse load, had to be granted again in 1268 to keep up this bridge at Fordingbridge, over the Avon in south Wiltshire.

The role of the king, whose income was, of course, enormous, could be more direct. In 1381, King Richard II donated his proceeds from Rochester fair back to the town to rebuild the timber bridge swept away in a flood the previous year. Rochester Bridge also illustrates the continuing role of the church as a property owner. In 1266-7, the Bishop of Rochester caused several houses and a wharf to be built and let, so that the proceeds could be used specifically for bridge repair. This arrangement continued until the quay was destroyed and the houses burned down in the siege of the town by the Earl of Warren and Roger de Laybonne.

The bridges under the direct control of monasteries, abbeys or local churches, would, of course, be maintained on the alms and donations culled from travellers, perhaps collected by the priest of the bridge chapel. Despite the ever-present influence of the church, the actual money collected very frequently found its way into private pockets, not to be used for its proper purpose at all. In 1334, for example, the parson of St Clement in Huntingdon petitioned Parliament about the proceeds from his little bridge chapel—*the keeping of which chapel our Lord the King has granted and delivered to Sir Adam . . . warden of the house of St John, and receives and makes away all manner of offerings and alms without doing anything for the repair of the said bridge or other said chapel which he is bound to do.*

The full authority of the Pope himself had sometimes to be invoked when those responsible would not fulfill their obligations. Thus, for example, Pope Sextus VI in 1473 had to instruct a Sussex prior to make good his neglect of:

The Chaple of St Mary, belonging to the Priory on a certain great bridge of stone on the highway between Bramber and Sele.

There were literally hundreds of similar instances.

Technical developments

The medieval era spanned several centuries, during which time there was little technical advance in the evolution of bridge types. The care and skills lavished on the building of the great cathedrals, were not, by and large, carried over to the construction of roads and bridges. Although many bridges were built robust enough to survive into the present day, they were originally built more for practical workaday purposes, than as uplifting symbols of man's urge to express his ideas about his world.

The shared characteristics of medieval bridges

tend to be short masonry arch spans bearing on heavy abutments and thick piers. Even though some medieval bridges are quite long overall, for example, Bideford Bridge in Devon, their individual arch spans tended to be less than 50 feet. So on long multi-span bridges the large number of piers necessary would frequently cause severe constriction of the river's flow.

The piers were usually heavy enough to act as abutments for each span, so that if one arch collapsed, those on either side would not be affected. This stability accounts for the variety of arch shapes in some medieval bridges. Radcot Bridge, for example, had its centre span destroyed in the battles between Richard II and his rivals. The central arch was subsequently rebuilt to a slightly different pattern.

Despite the generally weighty and static principles behind the medieval bridge, there were two significant steps forward in design. The first was the realization that bridge piers were better protected by triangular cutwaters on both the upstream and downstream sides, rather than on the upstream side only. The Romans had evolved the upstream cutwater, but left the downstream side square. The flow of water past the pier created eddies and small whirlpools downstream, which tended to erode and undermine the pier and its foundations. The addition of the downstream cutwater provided much smoother flow of water, and so reduced the wear. These cutwaters were often built right up to road level to provide recesses or refuges for pedestrians on the narrow roadway.

The second important construction feature evolved in medieval times was the ribbed arch. Typically, four or five rings of voussoir stones would be laid first on to the wooden scaffolding (the centering or falsework). Then, longer, flatter stones would be laid across these rings or ribs, to support the interior stones, or rubble infill. The use of ribs had two advantages; it significantly reduced the weight of the arch on the bridge foundations without sacrificing strength. It also reduced the amount of finely cut stonework (ashlar blocks) necessary, and thus saved time, cost and the amount of falsework. Ribbed arches were perhaps the only spin-off from the great age of cathedral building, in which the ribbed vault was often used.

Even though medieval bridges share many features, there is still a tremendous variety to be

Above left *The pointed arches of the Sturminster Newton Bridge over the River Stour in Dorset. The 'Gothic' arch was introduced to England by the Holy Crusaders in the Middle Ages so it may often be a useful guide to a bridge's age.*

Below left *The longest single medieval span in England—the Twizel Bridge in Northumberland over the River Till. The 90 foot ribbed arch is one of the few bridge structures to match the grandeur of contemporary cathedral architecture.*

Above right *The precise date of Fingle Bridge over the Teign on Dartmoor is unknown. The texture of the stone, the cutwaters carrying up to the recesses in the parapet and the strong but imprecise outline are marks of the medieval period.*

found among them. Medieval bridges were, after all, built in many parts of Europe, of many types of stone, in a variety of arch shapes, with their details—numbers of arch rings, styling of cutwaters, length of span—different in every case. What they share is the patina of age. They serve to remind us that in medieval times, travel was not easy on foot, horseback or cart.

Old London Bridge

Of all medieval bridges, Old London Bridge was surely the most famous. Although it was completed in 1209, its history stretched far beyond the medieval era, for it served the metropolis for over 600 years. Indeed, without the bridge, there would have been no metropolis. The growth of London spread outwards from the bridge point which, until 1894, was the lowest on the Thames. The bridge was at the intersection of the main road link to the continent and the east-west water trade route of the Thames. The bridge, therefore, focused an enormous amount of trade and business on the city of London, and the self-interested citizens effectively stopped any rival bridges being put up until the eighteenth century. Old London Bridge was a classic in every way and is the best example of virtually all aspects of medieval bridges.

Its building was supervised by a churchman, Peter of Colechurch, who possibly had inspiration from the Frères Pontiffes on the continent. Of course the bridge included a chapel built into it and, in its earliest days, there were also two defensive towers and one of the 20 spans was even a drawbridge. The funds for its building and maintenance derived from the Church, from the crown, from private bequests and from rents of houses and shops built upon the bridge itself. Its

enormously complex finances suffered the worst case of misappropriation of the period.

Like many medieval bridges, every one of its 19 pointed stone arches was a different size. Several were rebuilt completely and all were modified and extended in the bridge's long history. The river piers were very thick and their foundations rested on large boat-shaped 'starlings'—which offered very serious obstruction to the ebb and flow of the tide on the river.

The medieval bridge was not the first London Bridge. The invading Roman forces under Aulus Plautius gave the little hamlets of London and Southwark their first impetus, by erecting a Roman timber trestle bridge between them. This would not have been a great technical problem, since the sea level was some 12 feet lower then than now. Roman coins, pottery and the iron shoes from the piles themselves have been dredged up in a line across the bed of the Pool of London, showing the position of the bridge.

After the withdrawal of the Romans, however, there was a long silence until the tenth century when the *Anglo Saxon Chronicle* and the *Olaf Saga* describe a number of spectacular battles around a fortified timber bridge. The most interesting of these was that of 1014 when the English, under Aethelred, and the Northmen, under King Olaf, managed to recover Southwark from the Danes. Not until the bridge was destroyed, by the attackers rowing up to it, passing stout cables round the main piles and then rowing off with all their might, was it possible to win over the town. Such was the defensive strength of the bridge that even Duke William and the invading Normans in 1066 chose to go round via Wallingford rather than attempt to force the bridge at London.

After the Norman conquest, there are more

frequent references to the wooden bridge, mostly describing great fires, floods or storms tending to break it down. So frequent were the disasters that the Warden of the Bridge, Peter, Chaplain of St Mary Colechurch, decided that the only solution was to build a great, new, stone structure. In 1176, the work was begun, and for the next 33 years, Londoners watched the 20 spans grow across the 900 foot wide river.

The work proceeded one arch at a time, one perhaps every 18 months, each beginning with a foundation. A double row of posts was driven into the river bed to form a boat-shaped enclosure. Inside this 'coffer dam', elm piles were driven as far as possible below low tide level. It is thought that the irregularity of the arch widths was due to the problems of pile driving on the uneven river bed. After the spaces between the piles had been filled with loose rubble, chalk and gravel, planks of oak were laid over the piles and the bottom courses of ashlar masonry were laid in pitch on the planks. The carpenters would then move in to erect the wooden falsework on which to lay the carefully cut voussoir stones of each ribbed arch.

The money for all this work came from a great variety of sources. From the 1120s and 1130s, individual townsfolk had begun leaving bequests and rents to London Bridge, but the building of the great, new, stone bridge needed very much more than the income of the old. Henry II levied a special tax on wool to provide funds, leading to the legend that London Bridge's foundations were laid on woolpacks. The Archbishop of Canterbury and the Papal Legate donated 1000 marks and the cost of building the chapel was apparently borne by the senior mason who was 'The Maister Workeman of the Bridge'.

Peter Colechurch, sadly, did not live to see his project finished. He died in 1205, just four years before completion of the bridge and he was buried in the undercroft of the bridge's chapel.

The chapel was one of the first buildings on the bridge to be completed. It was dedicated to Thomas à Beckett who had been canonized in 1172 and who was very popular at the beginning of the thirteenth century. This was good for the bridge in that many pilgrimages to the shrine of St Thomas at Canterbury would cross the bridge, and it was thought that pilgrims and others would be very generous in their offerings to the memory of such a great man. The chapel was on the ninth pier from the northern or City end of the bridge, and had entrances both from the roadway and also from the river level for fisherman and mariners.

It is not known exactly what the original chapel, or indeed, the other buildings of the bridge, looked like when the bridge was finished in 1209. The houses were probably small and two-storied, the tower over the drawbridge was probably of timber and the stone gateway on the third pier from the Southwark side stood by itself.

However, we have a much clearer idea of the whole appearance by 1500. A journey across the bridge from Southwark to the City would have been a trip down a very busy medieval street. A traveller would have passed under the great stone gateway before gaining a clear view of the river and realizing the bridge had begun some 90 feet before. After passing more houses on either side, his steps would first have echoed over the wooden floor of the drawbridge and then within the great stone gate itself. Staring down from poles on on top of the gate would have been the severed heads of traitors and criminals. Then the traveller would have reached the thronging street beyond, with some of its houses overhanging to such an extent that the top floors were built right across the street from house to house. Emerging into the daylight again, he would see the Chapel of St Thomas of Canterbury on the right, now rebuilt in splendid perpendicular style. Perhaps he would pause and study the chapel, and, indeed, gaze at the rest of medieval London from this short, open stretch of bridge mid-river. He would continue

Below Old London Bridge in Elizabethan times, looking towards the City. The heads of executed traitors, murderers and thieves adorn the Southwark gateway and Nonesuch House perches next to the drawbridge span. The houses at the far end were burned down in 1632.

down the rest of the narrow street with houses, merchants and taverns on each side. In addition to the noise and bustle in the street, there was a continuous roar from the water below, as the River Thames rushed through the small arches, squeezed by the narrowness of the channels between the starlings.

Over the years, the rushing water below the bridge claimed many lives, both of people unlucky enough to fall from the roadway or houses, and of watermen unskilled or unwise enough to be capsized while shooting the bridge. The old proverb said 'London Bridge was made for wise men to get over and fools to go under'. But, apart from accidents, the bridge was a relatively healthy place to live, with the backs of the houses, at least, able to get plenty of fresh air and sunshine. The street itself was a good deal less filthy than the average medieval town street, since all household rubbish and soil went straight into the river, rather than building up in the open drains and gutters outside the houses. When the plague was raging through London in 1665, only two cases occurred on the Old London Bridge.

The other great hazard to life on the bridge was fire. During its entire history were repeated reports of conflagrations in the overhanging timber frame buildings. The worst was perhaps the earliest—in 1212—just three years after completion. A fire broke out at the Southwark end

and a crowd of spectators and helpers rushed on to the bridge from the City. The southerly breeze, however, carried sparks to the houses at the City end of the bridge and in no time the crowd on the bridge was caught between two huge fires. Those who were not burned, attempted to escape over the bridge parapet into some waiting boats, but the panic was so great that many were drowned as the small boats capsized. One early historian put the death toll of the disaster at 3000, but this is probably an exaggeration.

At the end of the century the bridge suffered a different kind of setback. In 1269, Henry III, who had problems with the loyalty of the Londoners, had given control of the bridge and its considerable income to his unpopular Queen, Eleanor of Provence. To the growing fury of the city, and those families and institutions which had bequeathed land or rents to the bridge for some years, she treated the entire bridge estate as her personal income. By 1281, there had been no cash for maintenance or repair for over ten years, so pontage was granted to the mayor, as an emergency measure, but it was too late. During the particularly hard winter of 1282, the river above the bridge froze solid and the great weight of ice bore down no less than five arches.

Not everything in the bridge's early history was disastrous, however. The bridge witnessed many happy occasions—the triumphal and very

Below *The end for Old London Bridge. Demolition began as soon as John Rennie's new structure on the left was opened in 1831. Removal of the great boat-shaped 'starlings' increased the river's scour and eventually caused serious problems for all the foundations of the other bridges in London.*

London Bridge through
the ages:
1: Around 1500: the
earliest records describe
the great stone gate at the
Southwark end (left), a
second stone gateway
guarding the drawbridge,
the chapel of St Thomas à
Becket rebuilt in
perpendicular style, and
large numbers of timber
houses and shops.

2: In the mid 1600s:
executed heads now adorn
the Southwark Gate, the
drawbridge gate has been
replaced by Nonesuch
House, the Dissolution has
reduced the chapel to a
warehouse and many houses
at the City end have been
destroyed in the fire of
1632. Waterwheels
appeared under the end
arches.

3: In the eighteenth
century, there were
many schemes which
were suggested for
improving the dilapidated
structure of the bridge.
Eventually, all the
buildings were removed,
the roadway was
considerably widened and
a large central span was
created by removing one
of the piers.

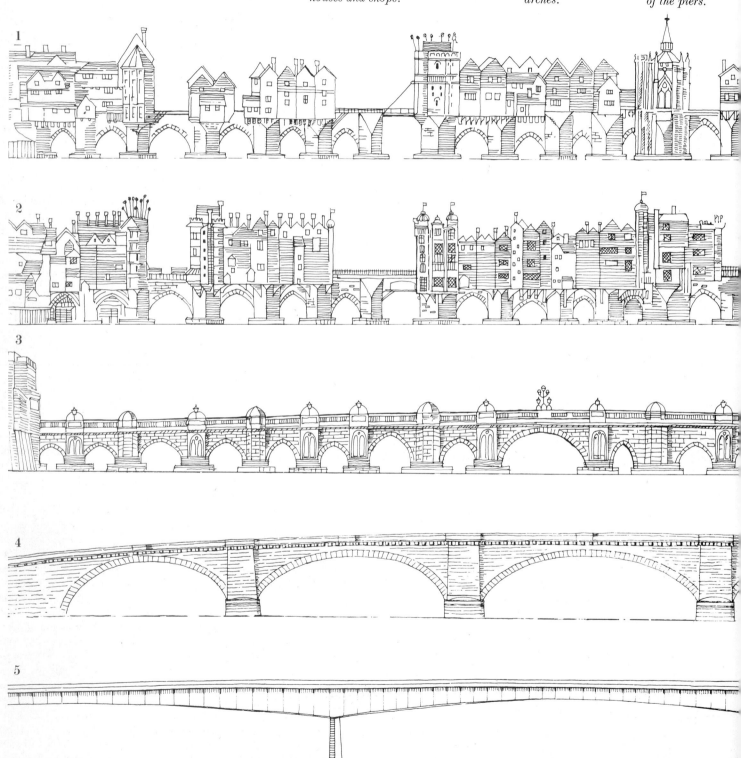

4: In 1831 John Rennie's New London Bridge (180 feet upstream) replaced the old structure with five semi-elliptical arches in stone. Although Rennie died before construction began, his son, Sir John, supervised the erection. Rennie's London Bridge survived until the 1970s when it was dismantled and sold to the United States.

5: Work started on the present London Bridge in 1968, alongside Rennie's bridge. Construction of the new pre-stressed concrete structure, and demolition of the old stone arches proceeded simultaneously without halting traffic. It was opened in March 1973 by Her Majesty Queen Elizabeth II.

spectacular processions on the return of the Black Prince after the battle of Poitiers, the welcome for Henry V after Agincourt, and later on, the state visit of Charles V, at the time, emperor of most of Europe. On such occasions, the bridge would be hung with lengths of fine cloths and other decorations; the merchants would arrange gaudy displays of their finest wares and speeches and songs of welcome would be declaimed at various points along the bridge. It was, after all, the main route into the city of London, from southern England and the continent.

This very fact, of course, made the bridge also liable to a certain amount of attack in those troubled times. 1381 saw the insurrection of Wat Tyler and thousands of peasants against the iniquitous poll tax of Richard II. Although the drawbridge was first raised against them, there was much sympathy in the city for the insurrection and when Tyler threatened to fire the bridge, he was allowed to pass.

In 1450, there was a furious battle running the whole length of the bridge between Jack Cade's men of Kent and Sussex and the Londoners, anxious to preserve the city from rebels. Later on, among other rebellions, there was that of Sir Thomas Wyatt in 1554, against the marriage of Mary and Philip of Spain. The bridge proved such an obstacle to his advance that he had to lead his forces into London from the west, via Kingston. Like the other rebellions, it failed.

It was usual for the heads or quarters of these rebels to be exhibited on the drawbridge gate on London Bridge. Both Cade and Tyler suffered this fate but Wyatt's remains were exhibited elsewhere. The gory remains were perhaps more distinguished and numerous in Henry VIII's time than at any other. Among the criminals, traitors and rebels were put up the heads of the Bishop of Rochester and Sir Thomas More (for refusing to recognize Henry as head of the Church of England) and Thomas Cromwell, Earl of Essex (for several reasons, including arranging the disastrous marriage between Henry and Anne of Cleves). Henry's unfortunate young wife of later years, Catherine Howard, although executed, did not feature at the drawbridge gate. Two of her favourites, however, Francis Dereham and Thomas Culpepper, were both exposed.

Old London Bridge, then, was at the heart of England's affairs, great and small, for six centuries. Immense changes and growth have taken place since the sixteenth century; the replacement of the drawbridge gate with the fabulous Nonesuch House in 1577; the water wheels, set in the end arches in about 1600, for milling corn and pumping water; the terrible fires of 1632 and 1666; the beginnings of decay and dilapidation in the eighteenth century; the row of elegant town houses put up by George Dance the Elder, to reverse the decline; the demolition of all the superstructures between 1759 and 1762; the final replacement of Old London Bridge with John Rennie's new five-arch wonder in 1831 (itself sold to the United States and replaced in 1973).

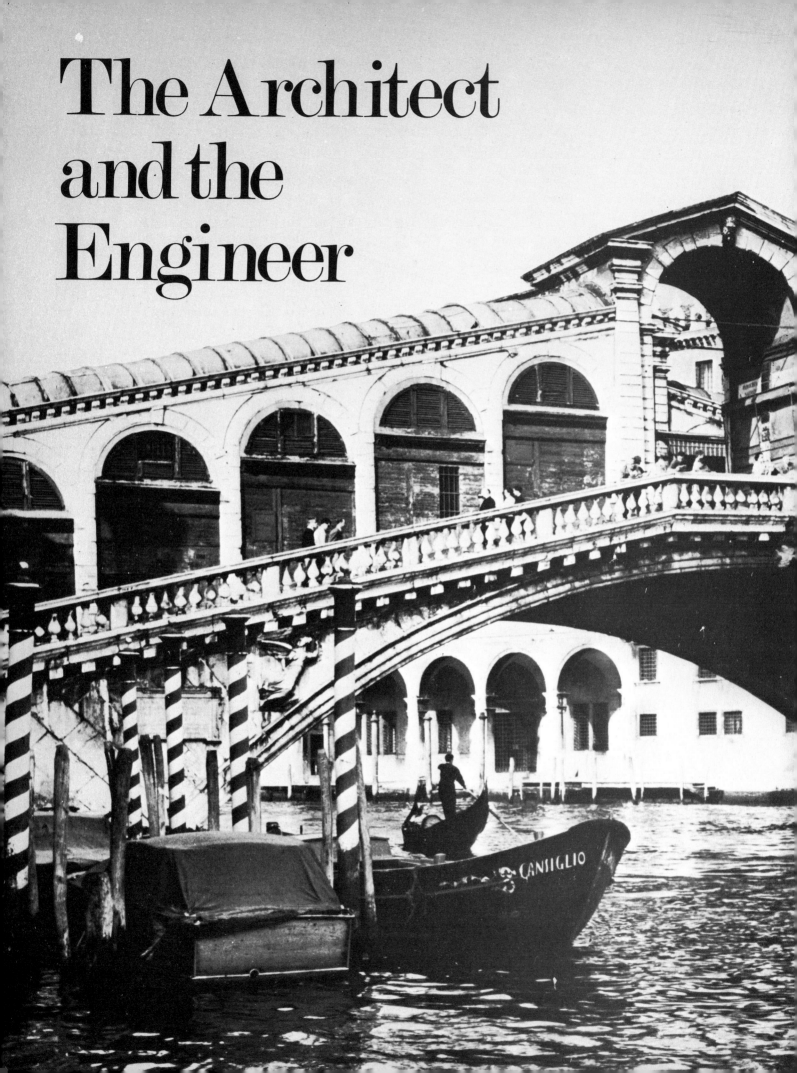

The Architect
and the
Engineer

Previous page *One of the finest structures of the late Renaissance is the broad segmental arch of the Rialto Bridge in Venice. Antonio Da Ponte's masterpiece was for years the only dry link across the Grand Canal separating the two halves of the city.*

THE NEXT ERA in building is one of transition. In building and construction there was a move away from the pragmatic approach of the jobbing medieval craftsman towards more scientific and theoretical methods. Two new types of men developed these methods; the architect, drawing his inspiration from Renaissance enthusiasm for the ancient classical world, and the embryonic engineer, putting to practical use the new sciences established by Galileo, Newton, and others. The period between the Medieval Era and the Industrial Revolution saw aesthetic refinements and technical improvements on existing practices and designs rather than radically new principles or materials. However, many beautiful and impressive bridges were constructed as the masonry arch was perfected.

The end of the medieval period was not a sudden event, but it was marked by two particular historical processes of the fifteenth and sixteenth centuries; the Renaissance spreading outward from its birthplace in Italy, and the Reformation in Northern Europe. The Reformation and the spread of non-Catholic churches spelt the end for the Church's authority in many aspects of life. The corruption of the Catholic church which led to the Reformation was expressed in both the terror of the Inquisition and the disgraceful sale of indulgences. Some bishops had actually used this form of spiritual blackmail to fund the construction or repair of bridges—parishioners would be released from their penance in purgatory for a period of time if they contributed to the bridge funds. Three English examples were Chollerford Bridge in Northumberland, Bideford Bridge in Devon and old Crawford Bridge across the Stour.

The new religious ideas, however, only had indirect effects on bridge making. By and large, members of the emerging middle classes became Protestants and the religious and civil wars which subsequently swept Europe were often an expression of the conflict between the new class and the old feudalism. Europe therefore experienced troubled times, like the Thirty Years war in Germany, and eventually the Civil War in England. Very little in bridge building was achieved and many bridges were destroyed. Those which were built were, for years, very similar in concept and construction to those of the Middle Ages.

The Italian Renaissance

In fifteenth and sixteenth century Italy, however, notions of art, science and man were in ferment. During the Renaissance, questions and answers were being sought and found, that would challenge established learning from another direction. Every aspect of knowledge was taken out and re-examined in the light of the rigorous aesthetic concepts of the ancient Greek and Roman cultures. This, of course, had implications in bridge building firstly in Italy itself, and then

Centre *Barden Bridge in Yorkshire was built in 1676 after the flooded River Wharfe had destroyed an earlier structure. Although the piers are heavy and the cutwaters extend to the parapet, the arch crowns are lighter and the whole bridge more symmetrical than medieval spans.*

Below *The construction techniques and designs of the Middle Ages died out gradually in Britain. Stopham Bridge over the Arun in Sussex dates from the time of Queen Elizabeth I. Its central arch was built high enough to allow the passage of river craft.*

later on, throughout the rest of Europe.

The Renaissance, however, was not sudden. The Ponte Vecchio, over the Arno in Florence, was built as early as the 1340s. Although its date is medieval, its most important structural feature is its segmental arch, very different from the Gothic or three or four centred arches of other medieval bridges. There is therefore, disagreement about whether the bridge should be classed as medieval or Renaissance. Taddeo Gaddi, who designed the bridge, has been called one of the great names of the Italian Renaissance.

A much greater name, Leonardo Da Vinci, does not appear to have been responsible for any stone bridges still extant. Bridge building, however, was one of the host of subjects to which he applied his mind. When he was seeking the patronage of Ludovico Sforza, he claimed:

I have a process for the construction of very light bridges, capable of easy transport, by means of which the enemy may be put to flight and pursued; and of others more solid, which will resist both fire and sword, and which are easily lowered or raised . . .

It is interesting to note that, even in the rarefied, intellectual atmosphere of the Renaissance, the strategic importance of bridges was still foremost in the minds of their constructors—particularly those built for the autonomous city-states of Italy. Da Vinci was, of course, the archetypal

Left *Jewellers, craft shops and houses line the roadway of the Ponte Vecchio. On the left, the Long Gallery links the Pitti and Uffizi Palaces.*

Below *The Ponte Vecchio in Florence was built in the 1340s. The three wide segmental arches, however, were far in advance of their time and foreshadowed Renaissance developments.*

Renaissance Man, with enormous talents both as an artist and as an engineer. Although today we think of these skills as very separate and specialized, this was not so in Renaissance times. Two bridges, particularly, illustrate this unity—the Ponte Di Rialto in Venice, and the Ponte Della Santissima Trinita in Florence.

The city of Venice is divided into two by the broad Grand Canal, and from the thirteenth until the nineteenth century it had only one bridge joining the two halves. This single crossing place was therefore crucial to the life of the city. Since the thirteenth century, the bridge had been a wooden one—trestles, with a drawbridge central span to allow masted boats to pass. In its early years this was known as the *Moneta*, or 'Money' bridge, as it was financed by tolls collected from the pedestrians who used it. Constructed of wood, however, it had to be rebuilt many times because of rot and fire damage. On one sad occasion, in 1450, the wooden structure collapsed when a great crowd had gathered on it to watch the pageantry of Emperor Frederick VII's state entry into the city. Despite such disasters, it was not until 1587 that the Venetian Senate decided to replace it with a more permanent, monumental stone bridge. A competition was held to find the best design and many famous names submitted plans including Scammozzi, Sansovino, Fra Giocondo, Palladio, Michaelangelo, and the

eventual winner, Antonio Da Ponte. Da Ponte was the Curator of Public Works at the time, and an old man of 75, but he went on, not only to complete the Rialto, but also to design the new Prison and the renowned Bridge of Sighs.

The foundations, in such a soft and marshy location, posed a problem. Da Ponte chose to drive many piles in, cap them below water level, and found his masonry abutments on an inclined plane to take the angled thrust at the end of the arch. This was such a novel idea that Da Ponte's enemies and rivals were able to stir up public doubts to the point when the Senate ordered an official inquiry, and work had to stop. The Senate heard the evidence of the designer, the builders, and even several idle Venetians who had gazed for hours on end at the four-man, mechanical hammer driving in the piles. The work was judged safe. The bridge was opened in July 1591, and to this day stands as Da Ponte designed it. In the month it was opened, a small earthquake caused pedestrians and shopkeepers on the bridge to panic, but on examination the structure showed not the tiniest crack.

The other great bridge of the Italian Renaissance was the Ponte Santa Trinità on the River Arno in Florence. Like the Rialto, it was built to replace an earlier timber bridge, the order for its construction being made in 1567 by the tyrant Grand Duke Cosimo I. His chief engineer,

Right above The two arms of the Pont Neuf were constructed at the turn of the seventeenth century to link the Left and Right banks of Paris across the Ile de la Cité.

Right centre and below Parisian bridges of the seventeenth century—the Pont Marie (centre) and the Pont Royal (below). The Pont Royal was the first bridge over the Seine with semi-elliptical arches. Both bridges were sponsored by wealthy aristocrats and court architects.

Below The unusual arch shapes of the Ponte Santa Trinità in Florence were devised in 1567 by Bartolomeo Ammanati. The elaborate escutcheons at the crowns disguise slight points in the shallow profile.

Bartolomeo Ammanati, is credited with its construction, although Michaelangelo is thought to have had a hand in the design.

The most startling feature of the Santa Trinità Bridge is the shape and the shallowness of the arches. In Roman and medieval bridge building, a wide span had to be correspondingly high to accommodate a full semicircle, like the fourteenth century Maddelena Bridge near Lucca. The Renaissance use of a segment of a circle meant that the ratio of rise to span could be reduced but even on the Rialto the ratio was one to four and the pedestrian paths on each side are steep enough to need steps. Santa Trinità boasts a ratio of one to seven. This ratio was made possible by using a unique curve. Two half parabolas were designed to meet at the crown at an obtuse angle and the slight point in the arch was disguised by a decorative escutcheon on the bridge face. It is thought that this shape was adopted on sheer aesthetic grounds, and it is a measure of the technical and engineering skill of the Florentines that such an original shape could actually be constructed. The bridge was tragically destroyed by the retreating German army in 1944, but it has since been rebuilt exactly to its original design.

The Renaissance in France

Italy was not alone in constructing impressive bridges in the sixteenth century. The Pont Neuf in Paris was built, with interruptions, between 1578 and 1604, to join the Ile de la Cité to the Right and Left Banks of the Seine. Building the two arms of the bridge, of five and seven arches respectively, was a massive civic undertaking, and collaboration between a large number of experts was necessary in the design stages.

Although important for the subsequent development of Paris, and although it occupies a special place in Parisians' hearts, from an aesthetic and structural point of view, the Pont Neuf did not represent a great leap forward. While the stonework of the arches, cutwaters and recesses was finely designed and executed, the semi-circular arch shape was not as adventurous as the Italian examples, and the foundations were so poor that they were giving trouble even before the bridge was opened. In the 1850s the Pont Neuf was extensively reconstructed.

Seventeenth century Paris saw two other notable bridges built, the Pont Marie and Pont Royal. The men behind these two projects were educated and wealthy aristocrats, close to the king. The Pont Marie was set up by Le Regrattier, 'treasurer to the Swiss', Poulletier, King Louis XIII's secretary, and Christophe Marie, contractor and builder. Pont Royal was designed by François Mansart an architect of Versailles, and Jacques Gabriel, whose son was later destined for fame in bridge construction. The Pont Royal was important for two reasons. It was the first Paris bridge to feature elliptical arches, and secondly it was the first bridge to use an open caisson to provide a dry working space on the river bed.

Design and style

Despite such technical improvements, the architect began to make his mark and develop a number of self-conscious 'styles'—classical, roccoco and baroque—which could be applied to any kind of structure. The bridges of the period reflect these different styles in their detailing—open balustrades sometimes replaced the solid parapets; niches for statues appeared within piers and abutments; voussoir stones were cut with chamfered edges to emphasize their pattern; decorative panels and Ionic columns adorned piers and parapets. Despite the great proliferation of styles and designs, some common threads link these bridges. Most arches were segmental; they tended to be lighter and slimmer, and consequently needed less massive piers and abutments than before; arch ribs virtually disappeared; multi-span bridges had each span carefully proportioned for maximum aesthetic effect.

In the seventeenth and eighteenth centuries, bridges came to be seen as a branch of art, more concerned with picture making, pleasing shapes and decoration, than with the expression of pure function. Nowhere was this more apparent than in England, on some of the great estates of the gentry's country houses. The most important influence here was the great sixteenth century Italian architect, Andrea Palladio, who had been instrumental in reviving interest in the architectural glories of ancient Rome. Palladio had actually drawn up several designs for bridges based on classical Roman ideas, and 200 years later some of these were adapted in England, notably at Wilton Park in Wiltshire.

The Grand Bridge at Blenheim Park was to have been the greatest of the English monumental and decorative bridges. Sir John Vanbrugh had planned a heroic structure to carry the estate road up to Blenheim Palace. The design, with three arches, towers, and a colonnade across the centre span, was calculated to reflect the heroic stature and the military achievements of the owner, the first Duke of Marlborough. The Duke's wife, however, who ran the estate in her husband's frequent and prolonged absences, saw the monumental design as a monumental waste of money, and continually frustrated Vanbrugh's passionate enthusiasm to get the job done. The Palace itself was not completed until after Marlborough's death in 1722—the bridge was never finished.

Several other great English architects designed bridges or at least were concerned with their

Centre *Thomas Grumbold's Clare Bridge along the Cambridge backs was built around 1640. The balustraded parapet came to be used on many decorative bridges but this example is thought to be the earliest in England.*

Below *A bridge proposed by the sixteenth-century architect Andrea Palladio. His interpretations and knowledge of classic Roman styles made him one of the foremost influences on the bridge builders of the next two centuries.*

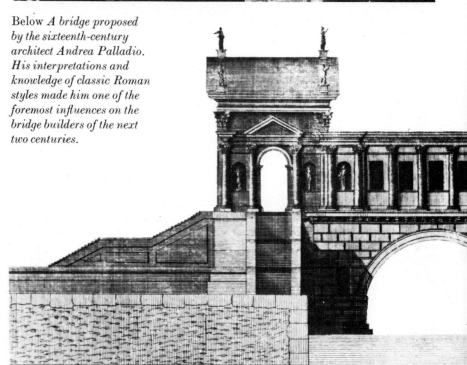

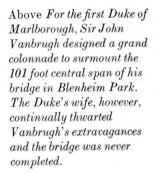

Above *For the first Duke of Marlborough, Sir John Vanbrugh designed a grand colonnade to surmount the 101 foot central span of his bridge in Blenheim Park. The Duke's wife, however, continually thwarted Vanbrugh's extravagances and the bridge was never completed.*

Centre *The archetypal English Palladian bridge, at Wilton Park in Wiltshire, was commissioned by the ninth Earl of Pembroke. Its proportions, roofed colonnade, balustraded parapet and rusticated voussoirs were copied on the estates at Prior Park, Bath and Stowe in Buckinghamshire.*

design. Inigo Jones is credited with Llanwrst and Bangor Isycoed bridges in Wales. Both Wren and Hawksmoor possibly had something to do with St John's Bridge in Cambridge and James Paine designed both the bridges at Chatsworth House and that at Richmond over the Thames. Robert Adam was behind Bath's Pulteney Bridge, the Aray Bridge at Inverary, and the decorative bridge at Kedleston Park, Derbyshire. Occasionally the decorative effect of bridges completely overtook their functional purpose. Adam himself made a detailed plan of a ruined bridge in 1768 for Bowood Park in Wiltshire, to look, in his words 'ruinous and in imitation of The Ancients'. Elsewhere, the general fashion for design and objects 'oriental' led to the construction of 'Chinese' bridges in wood, or, as at Sezincote House, Gloucestershire, a 'Hindoo' bridge inspired by the Elephant Caves of India. The most extreme example of bridges as decoration was perhaps the bridge put up in the grounds of Kenwood House, which looks genuine enough from the house, but when approached is quite unreal and two-dimensional.

In France, however, there had been developments of much greater importance. In 1716, the *Corps des Ponts et Chaussées* had been founded, an official government department responsible for advancing scientific road and bridge building, and for approving all plans for constructing the roads, bridges and canals of France. The first director of the Corps was Jacques Gabriel, son of the builder of Pont Royal. He led a distinguished team of graduates of the technical school, the *Ecole de Paris*. Just four days after the Corps was founded, it had its first opportunity to prove itself, when the ancient bridge at Blois was destroyed by the flooding River Loire. Gabriel and the Corps had produced plans within six months and contracts were signed within another three. The foundations alone took three years, construction of the 11 arches went on for another five. In 1724 Gabriel's masterpiece was opened for traffic and, despite being twice damaged in war, is still functioning.

Technology and engineering

It was then recognized that road making and bridge-building formed one branch of technical expertise. The Corps soon realized, however, that to achieve this expertise demanded a more thorough and disciplined approach than the *Ecole de Paris* could supply. Therefore the *Ecole des Ponts et Chaussées* was founded in 1747, to train young men in these particular branches of engineering. The first director was Gabriel's successor, the famous Jean Rodolphe Perronet. He was the son of a Swiss mercenary officer in the French army and his first preference was for a career in military engineering. The competition was so fierce for studentships at the Génie Militaire that he turned to architecture, and eventually did much to develop the concept of bridge building as a practical science. In addition to running the school, he developed a number of

Above *The 'Great' Bridge, at Chatsworth in Derbyshire was designed by James Paine in 1762 to match the grand style of the Duke of Devonshire's house and to blend harmoniously with the carefully arranged landscape.*

Centre *Robert Adam designed many bridges for the estates of the gentry. One of his best known is the Pulteney Bridge, complete with houses and shops, in the spa town of Bath. It was begun in 1769 under the patronage of Sir William Pulteney.*

useful bridge building machines, like water-driven pumps and mortar mixers, but most important by far were his contributions to bridge design.

Perronet realized that most of the thrust exerted by the increasingly shallow segmental arches was a horizontal force. Therefore, in a bridge with more than a single span, the horizontal thrusts of adjoining arches were equal and opposite. The arches could thus be used to hold each other up. Earlier bridges had needed heavy piers between arches to act as abutments and each arch was independent. In Perronet's designs, however, piers could become much slimmer—only needing to take the vertical weight of the bridge, the dead load—his arches were interdependent. The multi-span bridge therefore became a more dynamic and continuous kind of structure.

In practical terms, this idea had several implications. It meant that the amount of clear water beneath a bridge could be much greater, relative to the amount taken up in piers. Under the Old London Bridge, for example, the river was forced through gaps only one sixth of its total width. In some of Perronet's bridges the piers took up no more than one tenth of the river's width, leaving nine tenths of the waterway clear. Perronet took the light piers one step further by designing each pier as two columns joined by a lateral arch—making them lighter still.

His three best known works were the Pont de St Maxence over the River Oise, the Pont Neuilly over the Seine and the Pont de la Concorde in Paris. The Pont de la Concorde, begun when Perronet was 78, was to have been his finest work,

but, hampered by officialdom, he was forced to make his piers thicker than necessary, and solid, rather than in two columns. He was also instructed to raise the height of the arches by one metre. Even so, the bridge remains a dignified structure and a graceful complement to the Place de la Concorde which had been laid out between 1753 and 1770. Perronet died, aged 86, in 1794. He was living at the time in a shack at the end of the bridge, from which he could oversee the construction.

Perronet's bridges were more purposeful, their structure more closely bound to their appearance than many other works of eighteenth century architects. He was aware of the need for decorative features—the Pont de la Concorde has an open balustraded parapet, and a corbelled cornice, like the old Roman bridge at Rimini. But the decoration was not allowed to go too far. Originally the bridge was to have boasted statues on each pier but when the figures were put up it was thought that 'they distracted from the nobility of the bridge', and so were promptly taken down. The functional bridge form itself was judged to be aesthetic enough.

While Peronnet was developing the notion of bridge engineering as a discipline for study, a Welsh mason, William Edwards was discovering the craft for himself, by building some remarkable bridges. Born into a farming community in 1719, he continued a certain amount of farmwork all his life, but an early interest in dry-stone walls had led him to gradually more sophisticated masonry. By the age of 27 he had a considerable local reputation for his workmanship on the mills,

Below *The first major achievement of the* Corps des Ponts et Chaussées *was the bridge over the Loire at Blois, constructed between 1716 and 1724.*

forges and houses he had built. As a result, he was asked to build a bridge over the river Taff at what is now Pont-y-Pridd.

He put up a good bridge of three arches which were much admired for two and a half years after completion. However the regular floodwaters of the Taff, plus the fallen trees and debris in the river, proved too much for the arches, which collapsed one year when the flood reached parapet level. Edwards, who was under contract to maintain the bridge for seven years, was obliged to begin again. This time he designed a single, large arch (a 140 foot segment of a 170 foot circle), to avoid any piers obstructing the river's spate. But he had gone from too heavy to too light—the huge abutments and spandrels necessary for such a large span proved too heavy for the delicate crown of the bridge, which popped upwards and collapsed the whole arch.

Sticking to his plan for a single arch, Edwards was successful at his third attempt. This time he lightened the spandrels by piercing them with three circular tunnels on each side, nine feet, six feet and three feet in diameter. Not only did they make the bridge much lighter, but also they provided escape for floodwater and thus reduced the lateral pressure of the arch when the waters rose.

Pont-y-Pridd was completed in about 1755. It is a matter of conjecture whether Edwards devised the idea of reducing the bridge's dead weight with open spandrels himself, or whether he was aware of the practice having been used earlier. The Romans had lightened the river piers on one or two of their bridges with small arched openings, particularly in Spain. There had even been some medieval European bridges with arches through the spandrels. The fourteenth century Céret Bridge over the River Tech is thought to be one of the earliest in Europe. The Chinese, however, had solved the problem

centuries before, as shown by the handsome 117 foot arch of the An Chi Bridge in Hopei. Here the arches in the spandrels are large enough to emphasize the complete separation of supporting arch from supported roadway. This fundamental idea was taken up as later bridge building materials—iron and concrete—came into use, but was first used extensively by the bridge makers of the later eighteenth century.

Until this period, travel had still been on foot, horseback or in heavy unsprung coaches. Where roads existed, freight was moved about by wagon. Long-distance travel presented many problems, since routes were all unsurfaced, often with rutted hollows baked hard in dry weather and reduced to a boggy quagmire in autumn and winter. As neither fields nor roads were fenced, it was sometimes difficult to find the road at all.

In upland England, pack-horses were often the preferred method of shifting freight—wool, cloth, corn and even stone, lime and coal. In Yorkshire and Lancashire especially, are the remnants of bridleways of the pack-horse routes, dating back to medieval times. Bridges on these routes were still being built well into the eighteenth century. The bridge at Dob Park over the Washburn, near Harrogate, for example was put up in 1738. These bridges were constructed specifically for use by the pack-horse trains, and can be distinguished by their extreme narrowness—wide enough for a single file of laden animals.

This type of traffic, however, did not flourish for much longer, since from the mid-1700s, general road communications improved dramatically with the passing of the Turnpike Acts. Each one enabled landowners or private companies to construct properly surfaced roads and bridges, and to charge users a toll. While it took some time for the techniques of road surfacing to be fully developed by men like John Macadam, John Smeaton and Thomas Telford, the improved

Above Jean Rodolphe Perronet designed the Pont de la Concorde in Paris with interdependent arches so that the thrust from one arch could counteract that of the next. This technique required only slim river piers, but as construction began in 1788, Government officials spoilt the design by insisting that the piers be made more massive.

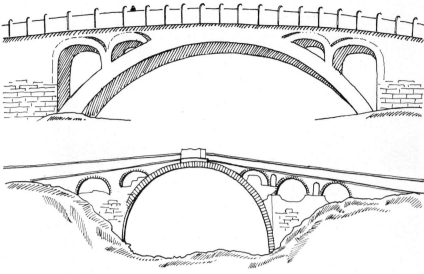

Left above and centre *Third time lucky—around 1755 William Edwards achieved the 140 foot span of Pont-y-Pridd after two failures. The holes in the spandrels both lightened the load of the arch crown and lessened resistance to the flood waters of the River Taff.*

Right above *Open spandrels in masonry arch bridges had been used long before they became popular in eighteenth century Europe. The An Chi Bridge (above) in Hopei, China, dates from the sixth century. The 147 foot span of the Céret Bridge (below) in France was built in the fourteenth century.*

roads and bridges speeded up traffic considerably. In 1754 a Manchester stage-coach company could make this remarkable boast:

However incredible it may appear, the coach will actually (barring accidents) arrive in London in four days and a half after leaving Manchester.

Transport was opened up further in this period by the beginning of the canal era. James Brindley's Bridgewater Canal in Lancashire was opened in 1761, to provide an outlet for coal from the Duke of Bridgewater's mines near Worsley. Canals rapidly established an efficient and cheap method of shifting heavy and bulky raw materials, and thus laid the foundations of the Industrial Revolution.

The implications of this general quickening of pace for bridge building were obvious. For example, handsome bridges in brick and stone sprang up for new roads at many places along the Thames; at Lechlade, Eynsham, Sonning, Henley, Maidenhead, Chertsey and Richmond—all displaying the fine architectural style of the period.

Timber bridges

However, the Renaissance architect responsible for the early development of the craft, Andrea Palladio, had developed other ideas of construction which had not been taken up with great enthusiasm. In his *Four Books on Architecture* of 1570, he had outlined several designs for timber truss bridges. Although he did not invent the truss, the idea had been applied in roof spans for centuries, he seems to have been the first to apply the king and the queen post systems to bridge-building. Palladio's most famous actual design

51

Above *Many types of pack-horse bridge were built between the Middle Ages and the advent of canals and railways.*

Centre *'Halfpenny Bridge' at Lechlade over the Thames was one of many toll bridges built in the eighteenth century in a period of profitable road building.*

Right *Eighteenth-century improvements to road systems included works carried out for military purposes. One branch of General Wade's road system in Scotland crossed the River Tay by Aberfeldy Bridge.*

was for a 100 foot bridge put up over the Cismone river. He claimed and demonstrated that truss bridges were economical to build and that they were capable of large spans, but could be made with short beams.

It took some 200 years, however, for these ideas to be utilized much. The next important timber bridges after Palladio's appeared in Switzerland in the eighteenth century. Hans Ulrick Grubenmann and his brother Johannes constructed timber bridges with spans around 200 feet at Schaffhausen, Richenau and Wettingen. They did not completely trust the simple truss form, and both relied on the arch as a fundamental structural form. The arch was the more widely used concept, even though the actual stresses in it are very much more complex to compute than in a truss. In England, Palladio's ideas had been loosely applied in one or two decorative structures, like the Mathematical Bridge of Queen's College, Cambridge and the 'Chinese' bridge of wood at Godmanchester.

It was in the United States that building in timber was to be more thoroughly exploited. With no long traditions of building in stone, the early American bridge makers used the most plentiful, economical and easily worked material. They produced some remarkable structures in timber during the early nineteenth century, while European builders wrestled with the problems and possibilities presented by the iron of the budding Industrial Revolution.

The first professional bridge builders in America were Timothy Palmer (1751-1821), Louis Wernwag (1770-1843) and Theodore Burr (died 1822). Like the Brothers Grubenmann, they all used a combination of the arch and truss. Palmer's best known work was the 'permanent' bridge carrying the Lancaster Turnpike over the Schuylkill River at Philadelphia, in about 1805. Its three arches were made up of three parallel frame ribs with the timber struts arranged to act like voussoirs. Louis Wernwag's Colossus Bridge in 1812, over the same river at neighbouring Fairmount, was a single 340 foot span, where the shallow arch of laminated timber formed the bottom chord of a superimposed truss for extra strength. Theodore Burr's system however, had the bulk of the load taken by a timber truss frame with a light arch running through the depth of the frame for strengthening. Literally hundreds of bridges were built to Burr's patent of 1817, although Burr's own structure over the Hudson at Waterford, New York, was one of the best known. The removal of the scaffolding in November 1815:

was a joyful moment to my brave fellows; and as you may well suppose, gave way to the impulse in loud and repeated Hurras.

These timber bridges were protected from the weather by planked sides and roof, and formed an important part of the American pre-industrial landscape.

The first modern truss design independent of the arch, was patented in 1820 by a Connecticut

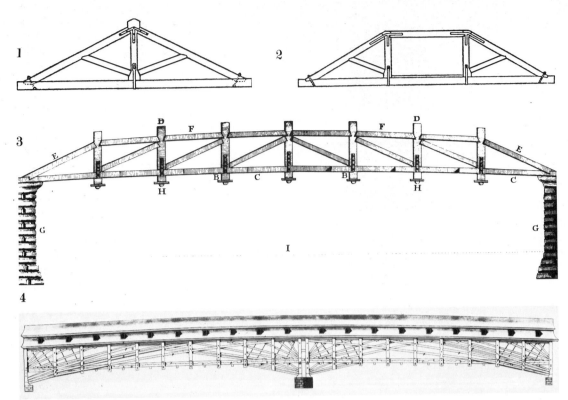

1

2

3

The evolution of the wooden truss:
Based on the ancient King and Queen post systems (1 and 2), Andrea Palladio had proposed a workable truss girder design in his architectural writings (3). However, subsequent wooden bridges tended to rely heavily on the arch as a basic structural form. In Europe the Grubenmann brothers achieved spans of some 200 feet (4) in the eighteenth century. Refinements came in the United States. Palmer's 'permanent' bridge of 1805 (5) and Wernwag's Upper Ferry Bridge of 1812 (6) were both built over the Schuylkill River and reached 194 and 340 feet respectively. With the Burr Truss system (7), patented in 1817, the arch was less important.

4

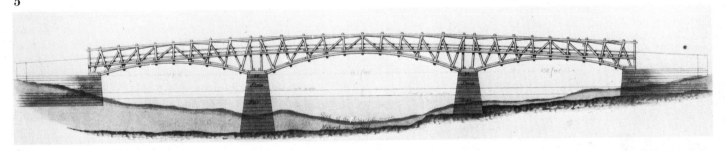

5

6

7

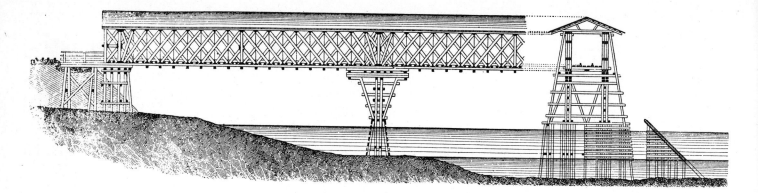

architect, Ithiel Town. The single or double web lattice was so straightforward to construct that local joiners and mechanics soon made it the most popular form of covered timber bridge. Through the 1840s, two other patent systems, the Howe and Pratt trusses, incorporated some iron tension bars in the truss frame and thus heralded the gradual displacement of timber as a bridge building material.

Before Europe faced the great changes of the Industrial Revolution, however, bridges of stone were reaching their finest development, and nowhere better illustrates this last era of stone building than London. For 500 years Old London Bridge had been the only bridge of the metropolis. Between 1750 and 1817, three new bridges were erected by the last of the great architect-engineers. Westminster (1738-1750) was designed by the Swiss engineer Charles Paul Dangeau Labelye, who, for the first time used open caissons rather than cofferdams to lay the foundations. Robert Mylne was responsible for Blackfriars Bridge (1760-1769). A hot controversy surrounded Mylne's and John Gwynne's competing designs

for this bridge, Mylne's being thought much too fancy and Gwynne's supporters calling him:
the puffing phenomenon, with his Fiery Tail Turn'd Bridgebuilder.
Mylne had recently returned from travelling in Europe, and incorporated both continental decorative ideas, like Ionic columns on the pier faces, and also Perronet's structural breakthrough—the interdependent arch.

Waterloo Bridge (1811-1817) had begun life as the Strand Bridge, when John Rennie had been asked to judge a design submitted by one George Dodd. He had rejected this design as being more or less a straight copy of Perronet's Neuilly Bridge, and was subsequently asked to submit a design of his own. Rennie had been designing bridges for 25 years and had built a great reputation for his work on steam grain mills, docks and especially canals. He belongs, therefore, in the next chapter on the Industrial Revolution, although Waterloo Bridge and New London Bridge (which eventually replaced Peter of Colechurch's structure), belong at the end of the development of the masonry arch.

Right above *London's second crossing was Westminster Bridge, designed by Charles Labelye and completed in 1750. The foundations were so unsteady that it had to be replaced a century later.*

Right centre *The massive arch rings of Blackfriars Bridge under construction in the 1760s. So strongly did the Thames flow after the removal of Old London Bridge that Robert Mylne's structure suffered the same fate as Westminster Bridge, and was replaced in the mid-nineteenth century.*

The Industrial Revolution

FROM THE LAST part of the eighteenth century, the process of industrialization began in Britain and gradually spread throughout the world, bringing huge changes in all aspects of living. New types of transport, canals and railways, developed alongside the steam engine and the ever increasing exploitation of coal. Cast and wrought iron offered new possibilities in machine making, building and construction. All together the new technologies needed new ways of organizing labour in larger urban communities. Growing towns added to the need for continual improvements in the transport system to carry more goods, foodstuffs and raw materials.

In these developments, two new kinds of professional can be seen—the 'civil' and 'mechanical' engineers. Men of prodigious talent, like Telford, John Rennie, the Stephensons, Brunel and many others, left their mark on the landscape in many ways. Among their most lasting memorials are the bridges they built using new principles, new methods and new materials.

Iron Bridge

There is some evidence that a Leeds iron-founder built a 72 foot iron arch at Kirklees in Yorkshire in 1770. But the bridge which is more often held to have begun the Age of Iron was built at Coalbrookdale, on the Severn Gorge in East Shropshire, England. The area has been called the 'cradle of the Industrial Revolution'. From the sixteenth century, coal had been mined there. By the mid-1700s there was also the thriving iron-smelting works of the Darby family and John Wilkinson. In addition there were potteries, tile and brickworks, all based on the rich deposits of coal, iron ore, limestone and clays of the neighbourhood. Local transport was by horse and cart and one or two local canals. Long-distance movement of finished materials was via sailing barges on the River Severn. While the river was essential for transporting cargoes out of the area, it seriously hampered the movement of coal, pig iron, clay and firebrick between

Previous page *The Iron Bridge over the Severn Gorge near Coalbrookdale heralded a century of bridge building in iron. The heavy stone abutments shown in this engraving of 1781 had later to be lightened because of their tendency to pinch the arch and raise the crown.*

Above *The Iron Bridge today, 200 years after work began. Although now closed to motor traffic, the 100 foot cast iron arch stands without major structural modification.*

Left *Joints in the bracing and ribs of the Iron Bridge arch echoed many techniques of carpentry with iron dovetails, dowells and wedges.*

the ironworks, mines and potteries within the area. In 1775 therefore, a group of local industrialists met to begin planning a single-arch bridge between Madeley and Broseley to solve this problem.

A Shrewsbury architect, Thomas Farnolls Pritchard, was commissioned to prepare the first design, and in a month he had come up with a plan for an iron structure, with four segmental ribs and a 120 foot span. For two years the design was debated and modified by Abraham Darby III, John Wilkinson and a group of local businessmen—Edmund Blakeway, founder of the Coalport China Works, Edward Harries, a local landlord, John Thursfield, the earthenware manufacturer and the Guest brothers, of a local mining family. Pritchard died in 1777 just after a definitive plan was settled and although it is still not certain how much he had to do with the final design, his contribution is thought to have been significant.

The decision to build in iron carried two advantages. It meant that the parts of the bridge could be cast on shore and erected without elaborate centering to obstruct river traffic and that the 100 foot span and 40 foot clearance would be adequate for both horse drawn and sailing barges.

Abraham Darby himself took charge of the construction. He enlarged his furnaces at Coalbrookdale to cope with the casting of the then massive 70 foot ribs for each half of the main arch. He supervised the building of the large stone abutments necessary to carry the roadway high over the river and he kept detailed records of the expenditure, down to the nine guineas spent on beer on October 23 1779 for the work force to celebrate the completion of the main structure.

The first large iron bridge in the world was opened on New Year's Day 1781, and was, from the start, a spectacle to be admired by all. The bridge proprietors exploited this aspect of their work by commissioning (for £29) the Haymarket Theatre scene painter, Michael Angelo Rooker, to produce drawings and engravings for sale to the admiring public. As the present Ironbridge Trust guide book puts it:

The bridge was more than just an important development in civil engineering. It was part of a sublime Romantic spectacle which helped to change the way in which artists, and ultimately other people, looked upon the achievements of Industry.

Despite the adventurous use of iron, however, the Iron Bridge was a conservative design—the designers drawing on known shapes and techniques of construction with other materials rather than devising radically new procedures for cast iron. The semi-circular shaped arch, for example, seems to hark back to the classical arch shapes of the Roman builders. Although perfectly suited to use with cast iron, the shape appears less adventurous even than Pritchard's first suggestion of a segmental profile. All the iron joints in the arches, radials and pillars, reflect practices of carpentry—there are dovetails, shoulder joints, and wedge fittings. The circular bracings in the spandrels echo the pierced spandrels then current in masonry bridges. However the fact that the arch is still standing probably owes much to the caution of Darby, Pritchard and the others in the handling of its design.

Canals

Water transport was fundamental to the development of the Coalbrookdale industrial community. In the latter half of the eighteenth century many other budding mining and manufacturing industries saw the need for a cheap system of bulk transport. Despite the turnpikes, roads were still

James Brindley's 'Castle in the Air'. The Barton Aqueduct carried Britain's first industrial canal over the River Irwell in Lancashire, and was opened in 1761.

bad enough to restrict long-range overland transport, especially for industries like the Wedgwood potteries whose products were often badly damaged in transit. Small canals and improvements to natural waterways had been built for centuries—Leonardo da Vinci is credited with the prototype of the familiar mitre lock in 1482. The first in England was on the River Lea in 1574, in France the Briare canal had linked the Seine and the Loire in 1642 and the Canal du Midi had linked the River Garonne at Toulouse with the Mediterranean in 1685. However the canals which contributed most to the Industrial Revolution in England began with James Brindley's canal for the Duke of Bridgewater in 1761.

The Duke, Francis Egerton, was concerned to develop his estate by finding a way to exploit 'a mountain of coal' on his land. He was fortunate in that the coal fired steam engines of Newcomen and Watt were then beginning development. The engines would eventually supply the badly needed motive power for the new industrial machinery which would thus stimulate a profitable trade in coal. Having visited the Canal du Midi, the Duke hired Brindley, a self-taught mill wright, to cut a canal between his mines at Worsley and the town of Manchester. Brindley's technique was to keep to one level by constructing his canals along contour lines to avoid building difficult bridges and aqueducts. However, one aqueduct he could not avoid was to carry the canal over the river Irwell at Barton. It was hailed as a marvel by contemporary observers. Brindley, whose genius was for surveying and engineering rather than spelling, was soon making an 'ochilor servey or ricconitoring' for a new 'novogation' to link the Duke's canal with Runcorn on the Mersey—a route in effect which joined Manchester to Liverpool and the sea. This too was an immediate success and canal mania began in earnest. Brindley himself planned the Grand Trunk canal to link the Mersey with the rivers Trent, Severn and Thames and although he did not live to see it completed, other great engineers took up the challenge and covered the country with a vast network of waterways. By 1840 2236 miles of river navigation had been improved and 2477 miles of canals had been dug. It was held that, south of Durham, no place in the country was more than 15 miles from navigable water.

The canals required hundreds of bridges of many kinds. Modest brick and stone arches carried existing roads over them. Small, balanced draw bridges were adapted from Dutch patterns to join farm tracks between adjacent fields. Roving bridges carried the towpath from one side of the canal to the other. The iron 'split bridge' with two separate cantilevered brackets evolved to allow boats to pass under, horses to pass over and their ropes to pass through without unhitching. In industrial areas, like Birmingham, many cast iron arches still carry the towpath over the hundreds of minor factory cuts and local spurs off the main channels. Lastly, the canals themselves often had to be carried in aqueducts for

Left above *Wooden drawbridges were often used where canals passed through low-lying fields. This example spans the Llangollen Canal.*

Left below *The canals themselves facilitated iron production by providing cheap bulk transport for raw materials. Standardized cast iron arches like this at Newbold, England, became common on the canals.*

Right above *Roving bridges carried the towpath to the opposite bank. Although many were built of brick and stone, Telford's Oxford canal has several iron spans.*

Right centre *The bridge at Great Haywood Junction where the Staffordshire and Worcester Canal meets the Trent and Mersey Canal. Brick arches were used for hundreds of accommodation bridges in the Midlands.*

Right below *A split bridge on the Stratford-on-Avon Canal, allowing the tow-rope to pass through the bridge without unhitching the horse from the barge where the towpath changes sides.*

Above Coldstream Bridge over the River Tweed was designed by John Smeaton, one of the first all-round 'civil engineers'. The sealed tunnels above the piers reduced the amount of redundant stone in the bridge.

some distance over river valleys and roads.

The engineers who laid out the canals needed a great array of talents. They were responsible to the canal companies for surveying the routes, for designing the locks, building bridges and tunnels, ensuring their plans were properly carried out by contractors and for doing a great deal of what we would now call public relations and committee work on behalf of their projects. Some of the canal builders were specialists like Brindley himself. Others were among a new breed of designers who called themselves 'civil engineers' for whom canal-building was but one of their many activities. These were men like William Jessop (1745-1814)—responsible for the last link in the great 'cross' of English waterways, the Grand Junction Canal. His other works included the West India Docks, Bristol Docks and a profitable iron foundry.

The term 'civil engineer' had first been used by John Smeaton (1724-1792) to describe himself. He planned the Forth and Clyde canal, built bridges at Perth, Banff and over the River Tweed at Coldstream, advised on the Old London Bridge, built Ramsgate Harbour, and is best remembered as the designer of the third Eddystone Lighthouse. Two men, however, achieved even greater renown for the range and versatility of their engineering works, particularly bridges. They were John Rennie (1761-1821) and Thomas Telford (1757-1834), 'the father of civil engineering'. The lives of both men spanned the canal era

and both gained large reputations for their work in canal construction and bridge design. While both used iron and stone, in Rennie's bridges the masonry arch was carried to perfection, while Telford explored the new ideas and possibilities offered by iron.

John Rennie

John Rennie was the youngest son of a farmer in East Lothian, Scotland. By the age of 12 he had exhausted the knowledge of his parish school teacher and, at his own request, was apprenticed for two years to Andrew Meilke, a mill wright on the Rennie's farm. Friends of the family enabled him to study at high school in Dunbar, where he demonstrated a remarkable talent for mathematics and 'natural and experimental philosophy'. He returned to Meilke's wrightshop as an assistant and developed such an extensive and profitable business that he was able to pay his way through Edinburgh University by 1783 and to tour England to study buildings and engineering works. He visited the Bridgewater Canal, and in Birmingham met James Watt who was developing stationary steam engines. Having set up his own mill wright business his first important job was the installation of the first steam driven grain milling machine at the Albion Mills, for Boulton and Watt. Rennie built his first bridge at the age of 23 over the water of Leith near Edinburgh in Scotland.

His major works were a number of canals and no less than three London Bridges, but he also built several mills, docks at London and Holyhead, he supervised the draining of the Lincoln and Cambridge fens and designed the Bell Rock Lighthouse. His Kennet and Avon canal, opened 1799, linked the Thames with Bath and features the handsome Dundas Aqueduct over the Avon in the Limpley Stoke valley. Otherwise Rennie built few of his canal bridges himself, although the canals themselves were great works. For example, between Rochdale and Todmorden, locks carry the waterway right over the Pennines.

Rennie's stone bridges were more successful than those he built in iron. His first major work had been the design for Kelso Bridge, completed in 1803. It features five semi-elliptical spans of 72 feet with each pier decorated with a pair of Doric columns from cutwater to cornice. When he came to plan the 'Strand Bridge' over the Thames in 1811 he adapted the same design on a grander scale—the Act of Parliament for the change of name to 'Waterloo Bridge' specified the design should be *a work of great stability and magnificence* and should *transmit to posterity the remembrance of great and glorious achievements.* The bridge was opened in 1817 by the Prince Regent attended by the Duke of Wellington. Rennie was offered a knighthood which he declined, and Canova the Italian sculptor hailed the bridge as *the noblest bridge in the world, worth a visit from the remotest corners of the earth.*

In the construction of the bridge, the most important technical development had been the centering method. The massive wooden framework for each arch was constructed on shore and floated out into position. When the arch ring of voussoirs was nearly complete, the keystone was driven in hard enough to relieve the pressure on the centering. This made the 'fit' of the stones even tighter, so that when the framework was gradually slackened, ten days later, the 'sinking' of the arch was minimal—in fact less than three inches.

Two years later, Rennie's Southwark Bridge was opened. At the time, this was the largest cast-iron bridge constructed. The two side spans were 210 feet and the third centre span, was 240 feet, rising 40 feet above high water mark. It was constructed from hollow cast iron boxes shaped like voussoir stones and held together with an elaborate system of bolts, wedges and dovetail joints. Although, for its time, the design and construction were very advanced, in use, the bridge suffered from having narrow, steep approaches, and also from the imposition of tolls. Although it was more popular after the City of London freed it from tolls in 1868, it was eventually replaced in 1921 with the present Southwark Bridge.

Many of Rennie's ideas and construction techniques used on Waterloo Bridge were repeated in the construction of his last great design, the New London Bridge. In 1821 Rennie reported to the City of London Corporation that their plans for

Left *John Rennie built mills, canals, docks and iron bridges, but is best remembered as the last great designer of monumental bridges of stone.*

rebuilding the Old Bridge yet again were not economically viable and he tendered his own design for a replacement. His report was accepted, but he died—of overwork—before construction could begin. Many other designs were then considered, including an amazing proposal from Thomas Telford for a single cast iron span of 600 feet, but eventually Rennie's original plan was adopted. Rennie's son, John, was chosen to oversee the bridge's construction, and there were elaborate ceremonies both at the laying of the foundation stone in March 1825, and at the opening of the bridge in 1831 by King William IV and Queen Adelaide.

Below *Near Bath, the now defunct Kennet and Avon Canal crossed the River Avon in Rennie's fine Dundas Aqueduct, completed in 1802.*

Old London Bridge was then taken down. Since it had acted as a dam on the river, it had slowed down the ebb and flow of the tide. With the removal of the piers and starlings the river bed above the Old Bridge was immediately subject to increased scour from the unobstructed water. Foundations on Labelye's Westminster Bridge, Mylne's Blackfriars Bridge and even eventually Rennie's own Waterloo Bridge, began to weaken, and all had to be replaced.

Thomas Telford

Thomas Telford revolutionized 'civil engineering'. He was liked and respected by all, from his wealthy patrons to his own labourers. He had a huge thirst for knowledge in all practical arts and sciences, and even wrote passable poetry.

He was born in 1757, the only son of a tenant shepherd, near Westerkirk in Dumfrieshire. His father died the year Thomas was born and in his early years he was cared for by his mother and the equally deprived neighbours and relatives in the parish. By his early teens, he had learned to read and write at the local Parish School, and chose to become appriticed to a stone mason rather than start working as a farm labourer. His first employer treated him so badly he ran away, but Thomas was able to continue his apprenticeship through the influence of his mother's cousin, the land steward on the neighbouring estate of Sir James Johnstone. Telford soon progressed from apprentice to journeyman and was kept busy building small bridges, improving roads,

Below *When it opened in 1819, the first Southwark Bridge over the Thames was the largest iron structure of its time. John Rennie designed hollow iron boxes for the three arches spanning more than 200 feet each.*

Left above *John Rennie died before work on his last great design could begin. The construction of New London Bridge was supervised by his son in the late 1820s.*

Left centre *London Bridge in the 1920s. Having lasted over 140 years, the bridge was sold in 1970. Reconditioned London buses now sell ice creams to visitors on Rennie's bridge re-erected over an artificial lake in Arizona.*

Below *Telford's staggering proposal for a cast iron replacement for Old London Bridge. Although engineers today believe it would have been quite practicable, its 600 foot span was too daring for the City sponsors.*

Right Thomas Telford, the Father of Civil Engineering.

Below Telford's first important bridge as County Surveyor for Shropshire was this sturdy stone structure to carry the Holyhead road over the River Severn near Shrewsbury. Some 20 years after the bridge, Telford began the survey and improvement of the entire London to Holyhead route.

Right Throughout his career, Telford designed many stone bridges in England and in his native Scotland. One of his last and largest was the Dean Bridge over the Water of Leith in Edinburgh.

cottages and farm buildings around Langholm on the estate of the Duke of Buccleuch. At the same time, he read a wide selection of books from the library of local spinster, Miss Palsey, who had taken a liking to 'laughing Tam'. He was particularly impressed with Milton's *Paradise Lost*.

Gradually, however, the work around Langholm dried up and Telford went to work in Edinburgh on building the New Town for two years. He studied and drew all the great buildings of the city, but eventually decided to make for London, where his industry and ambition would be better rewarded. Through his contacts with Miss Palsey's brother, he first obtained a job as a mason on building Somerset House. Later, through his contacts with the Johnstone family, he won the patronage of Sir William Pulteney, and worked his way up from building foreman on the Portsmouth Docks, to Sir William's architect on his Shropshire estates. When he was about 30, he was appointed as County Surveyor to Shropshire and began his extraordinarily prolific design work on bridges, roads and canals.

During his lifetime, Telford was responsible as County Surveyor for some 42 road bridges in Shropshire, most of them in stone. He had already built the Montford Bridge carrying the Holyhead road over the Severn in 1790, and went on to design the graceful Bewdley Bridge over the same river in Worcestershire. Throughout his life Telford built many other bridges in stone, many of which had innovations or distinctive features. The 112 foot span of the Tongueland Bridge over the Dee (1805), for example, had parallel internal spandrel walls, rather than mere rubble infill; the Over Bridge in Gloucestershire had a 150 foot arch splayed in the manner of Perronet's Neuilly Bridge; the Dean Bridge at Edinburgh had hollow piers to reduce weight, and a double row of arches.

But it was for his pioneering work with iron that Telford was chiefly remarkable in the history of bridge building. There were four major responsibilities Telford carried in his life. In addition to being County Surveyor for Salop, he was, in the words of his contract 'general agent, surveyor, engineer, architect and overlooker' for the Ellesmere Canal Company. As engineer to the British Fisheries Society, he was responsible for a huge development project involving roads, canals, bridges and harbours to revitalize the Scottish Highlands. He also oversaw the surveying and construction of an improved road between London and Holyhead. Each of these projects incorporated at least one iron bridge.

During the 1780s and 90s many experiments in iron bridge building were made, in addition to Telford's works of the period. One of the most notable was a 236 foot span over the River Wear at Sunderland, built by Rowland Burdon and Thomas Wilson. It has long been believed that this bridge was designed by the radical American, Tom Paine, whose writings Telford is said to have admired. Paine did take out a patent for a system of building bridges of iron, and a trial prototype of his patent was cast and erected for the admiring public at 'The Yorkshire Stingo' public house in Paddington. However, Paine left England for revolutionary France before the Sunderland plan was confirmed. The only connection between his prototype and Burdon and Wilson's improved erection at Sunderland appears to be that they were both cast at Walkers Foundry at Rotherham and it is not impossible that some of Paine's bridge was in fact melted down for the Wearmouth span in 1796.

In the same year, at Buildwas in Shropshire, Telford put up his first iron bridge which was cast by the Coalbrookdale Company. Compared to their nearby Iron Bridge, Telford's bridge contained half the amount of iron in the structure, even though the span was 30 feet greater. As with the Iron Bridge, the main problem was to span the River Severn in a single arch so as not to interfere with river traffic. Although it was replaced with the advent of heavier road traffic, Telford's first iron bridge was successful enough to encourage him to use the material more and more.

His next use of cast iron was for a small aqueduct at Longdon-on-Tern to carry the Shrewsbury Canal in an iron trough 180 feet over a little valley. When he came to construct the two major aqueducts of the Ellesmere Canal he was able to use similar iron troughs which, relative to the only other alternative of stone and puddled clay, were very light. The Chirk Aqueduct over the Ceiriog was built mostly of masonry, but with iron linings for the canal, and was opened in 1801, although actually designed in 1794-1795. Four years later, the magnificent Pont Cysyllte was opened. In this case, only the 127 foot piers are masonry. Between them, arches of cast iron plates carry the iron trough over 1000 feet across the valley of the River Dee. Although the Ellesmere Canal itself was not finally executed as the Company and Telford had planned, Telford's professional reputation was now absolutely secure.

It is not possible here to describe fully the scope and detail of Telford's proposals for the road network, the Caledonian Canal, the harbour works and the many bridges in the master plan for his native Scotland. Beginning in 1801 Telford spent 20 years surveying, designing and organizing the work. However, one small bridge in the huge undertaking is particularly worth singling out. A cast iron arch carries the A941 trunk road over the River Spey at Craigellachie. The bridge, built between 1812 and 1815 was a useful step forward in bridge design, employing, as it did, the concept of minimum materials for maximum strength in the diagonal bracing of the concentric arch rings. This gives the bridge the modern appearance of a trussed arch.

Telford's other major overland route was the London to Holyhead road. A board of Parliamentary commissioners had been appointed at the insistence of Irish members of Parliament to improve communications with Ireland. Telford

Above *In 1796 Rowland Burdon and Thomas Wilson had completed Britain's second important cast iron span—the bridge over the Wear in Sunderland. The main arch ribs consisted of modular units of iron struts and provided a clear span of 236 feet.*

Centre *Telford pioneered the iron trough aqueduct with this 180 foot structure for the Shrewsbury Canal at Longdon-on-Tern.*

67

surveyed an improved route for the road, he devised a solid and hardwearing technique of surfacing and maintaining the road, and he designed a number of elegant roadside toll houses. The Welsh section of the road, including the unique Bettws-y-Coed bridge, was improved in just four years, although it took 15 years to complete all the improvements. The one major obstacle in the whole route was the stretch of water between the mainland of Wales and the island of Anglesey. To solve the problem of bridging the Menai Straits, Telford used a principle of construction whose development was still in its infancy—the suspension bridge.

The Menai Bridge

The early history of iron suspension bridges is rather obscure. The earliest European suspension bridge in iron seems to have been the Winch Foot bridge at Middleton in Teesdale, built in 1741 for local lead miners. Its span was 39 feet, and its 2 foot wide floor rested directly on the iron chains. After the development of a method of producing wrought iron with heavy rollers in the 1780s however, the principle of suspending a level roadway from hanging chains became feasible. In the United States, a Pennsylvania judge, James Finley, patented a system for producing this type of bridge in 1808. Over the first two decades of the nineteenth century, some 40 bridges were put up to his designs, notably at Jacob's Creek in 1801, at Dunlap's Creek in

Pennsylvania, and at Newbury Port over the Merrimack River in 1810.

In Britain, John and Thomas Smith had put up a 216 foot suspension footbridge over the Tweed at Dryburgh in 1817, but more notable was the work of Captain Samuel Brown, RN (1776-1852) who had developed improved methods of producing iron chains, both for use in the Navy, and for the construction of suspension bridges. His best known achievements were the Union Chain Bridge of 1820, again over the Tweed, near Berwick, and the famous Chain Pier at Brighton.

In 1816, however, Captain Brown and Thomas Telford had developed such similar ideas that they had decided to work together on plans for a 1000 foot suspension span over the River Mersey at Runcorn. Although sufficient funds to build this giant could not be raised, Telford's design and Brown's tests on wrought iron eyebars proved very valuable when Telford came to work out his proposal for the Menai Straits.

Many architects and engineers had submitted ideas for bridging the Straits, among them, was John Rennie with a proposal for a three-arch bridge of iron. All the plans had been turned down by the Admiralty who insisted on enough head-room for the Navy's tallest fighting ships and on a clear channel during construction. Telford's eventual plan provided 100 feet of vertical clearance above high water, and a 550 foot wide channel. The Holyhead Road Commissioners approved the plan and work began in 1819.

The seven high stone arches to carry the road

Left below The Pont Cysyllte Aqueduct was completed in 1805 and still carries the Llangollen Canal over 1000 feet across the Dee valley.

Right above Telford's Waterloo Bridge on the London to Holyhead road at Bettws-y-Coed. Above the inscription, cast iron roses, thistles, shamrocks and leeks decorate the spandrels.

Right centre The chain pier at Brighton was designed by Captain Samuel Brown RN who did much of the development work for eyebar suspension chains. The pier was destroyed in a storm in 1836 by the same process that caused the Tacoma Narrows collapse a century later.

Right below Craigellachie Bridge was built in 1815 over the River Spey in Scotland. This iron arch was just one of the links in the 1000 mile road system for the Highlands' development, surveyed and supervised by Telford between 1801 and 1820.

from the shore to the towers, and the towers themselves, were constructed over the next four and half years. The two main piers were designed and built with extreme care. Telford thought a solid tower with rubble infill would just be 'a heap of rubbish', so he designed them hollow, with cross walls inside. The masonry blocks thus had to be cut and laid as well their inner as on their outer faces. In addition, many of the most important blocks were bound together with iron dowels.

Since nothing on this scale had been put up before, the wrought iron links for the main chains were thoroughly tested. The nine foot long links failed at 87 tons of tension. Each one was tested to 35 tons which was double the expected load. While under stress, the links had also been struck with hammers. Telford also erected a complete chain over a neighbouring valley to compute the pull necessary to haul it into position. When the masonry had been completed in 1825, the iron chains were erected.

First the side chains were stretched from the rock anchorages on each shore to the pylons. On April 26 a great crowd gathered to watch the hauling up of the first chain of the main span. A 400 foot string of barges floated the chain into position; one end was joined to the anchoring chain dangling over the Caernarvon pylon, the other was attached to tackle for hauling up to the top of the Anglesey tower. Some 150 labourers trudged around a capstan, and a great cheer went up as the chain swung free of the barge. In all, it took a tense hour and 35 minutes to raise and pinion the 21 ton chain in position. While cheers rang along the shores and three workmen scrambled across the 590 feet between the towers, Telford himself is reported to have been found on

his knees offering thanks. He had not slept properly for weeks and despite all his care, had suffered a great anxiety over the possibility of the chain's failure. However, by July, the other 14 chains were in position and the bridge was opened with great celebration on January 30, 1826. At 579 feet it was the longest span in the world.

In the next decade or so, many other eyebar-suspension bridges were put up, drawing on Telford's principles and experience with the Menai Bridge. In England, William Tierney Clark was responsible for the first Hammersmith Suspension Bridge in 1827, and Marlow Bridge in 1832. Eventually Tierney Clark designed the famous 660 foot span bridge over the River Danube in Budapest, which was first used in 1849, not by the general public but by a retreating Hungarian Army. At Fribourg in Switzerland, French and Swiss engineers developed the idea of using wire cables instead of chains. In 1834 they opened a bridge which took over the title of the longest span from Menai.

In 1829, towards the end of Telford's life, he was asked to judge a design competition for a bridge to span the Avon gorge near Bristol, an idea that only became feasible with the advent of the iron suspension bridge. Among the designs submitted was a proposal from the young Isambard Kingdom Brunel, for a suspended span of 913 feet, slung, without anchoring chains, from two solid towers high on either side of the gorge. When Telford rejected this along with all the other proposals, he submitted a design of his own, and another competition was announced, this time with Telford as one of the entrants. His proposal was for a bridge suspended from two monstrous, Gothic-style towers built up from the floor of the gorge. Public outcry followed the acceptance of his plan, and the Bristol magistrates decided instead to adopt the latest of Brunel's four submitted ideas.

When the final decision was taken in 1831, Brunel was barely 25 and Telford was in his seventies. The competition result was a kind of symbolic watershed. Telford, builder of roads and canals, was bettered by Brunel, who was to go on to engineer the Great Western Railway. In his latter years, Telford saw the start of steam railway transport. Capital for canals dried up as investors switched to railways which began the long process of drawing the traffic off the canals. With the advent of steam-powered ships, Telford's Great Caledonian Canal became obsolete; even his roads were, for a century or so, destined to be overtaken by rail.

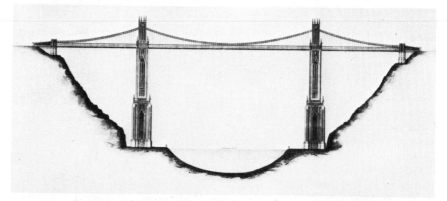

In Telford's lifetime, the idea of the 'civil engineer' became established as a member of a specific profession with a particular type of responsibility which he should discharge by working to certain high standards. The Institute of Civil Engineers was the formal expression of those ideals and it was fitting that in 1820, Thomas Telford was invited to become its inaugural President. He died in 1834 'full of years and honours' and was buried in Westminster Abbey.

Left above *The original wrought iron chains of the Menai Bridge. They lasted in this configuration until heavier and larger traffic forced their replacement with four chains of high tensile steel in 1939.*

Left second *William Tierney Clark built several eyebar suspension bridges, all very similar in design. This one, the original Hammersmith Bridge of 1827 over the Thames, was dwarfed 15 years later by his 663 foot span over the Danube in Budapest.*

Right above *The Menai Bridge carrying the London to Holyhead road across the Straits to Anglesey, was constructed between 1819 and 1826.*

Right centre *The 327 foot span of the Conway Bridge was completed a few months after the Menai Bridge in 1826, and it used the same principles.*

Left third *Telford's only lapse was in old age when he made this fanciful design for a Gothic suspension bridge over the Avon Gorge, near Bristol.*

Left below and right below *One of several proposals by the young Isambard Kingdom Brunel was eventually chosen for Clifton in 1831. Although work began in 1836 on the towers for the 702 foot span, a variety of factors held up construction for more than 20 years. Always one of Brunel's favourite and grandest projects, the delays in construction caused him considerable frustration. It was not until after Brunel's death in 1859 that his engineering colleagues completed the structure in recognition of his talents and achievements. The Clifton bridge, therefore, is not exactly as Brunel intended it to be.*

Railways

Previous page *In North America timber was cut from surrounding forests to build trestle viaducts for the pioneer lines. Here a wood burning locomotive is shown on the west slope of the Cascade Mountains in 1885.*

Right above *George Stephenson, whose work on steam locomotives and railway construction laid the foundations of a new era of communications.*

Right below *Robert Stephenson, engineer and railway mogul, built successful locomotives, surveyed thousands of miles of track, designed several famous bridges and died a millionaire.*

FOUR YEARS BEFORE Telford died, the railway era began in earnest with the opening of the line between Liverpool and Manchester. The success of the Stockton and Darlington railway of 1825 demonstrated the practical profitability of hauling freight and, later, passengers with a steam locomotive. The concept of the locomotive had been evolved from the stationary engines used for milling and pumping, winding and blowing in mines and ironworks since the late 1700s.

After 1830, steam railways began to grow in Europe and the United States, but in these early years, the important developments in locomotive building, track laying and bridge construction all happened in Great Britain. The railway engineers had to solve all manner of novel problems with very little precedent to guide them. They had to be practical, inventive, daring and ruthless to achieve their results. Although there were hundreds of individuals in this new breed of engineer, the achievements that stand out are those of father and son, George and Robert Stephenson, and the latter's contemporary, Isambard Kingdom Brunel.

George (1781-1848) and Robert (1803-1859) Stephenson

George's father was a fireman of a pumping engine at a colliery of Wylam near Newcastle. George spent a hard childhood doing odd jobs and learning to assist his father at the engine. At 14 he was appointed fireman in his own right. He learned to write at a village night school when he was 18, and began to study mathematics a year later. George's wife died in 1806 and his father had been blinded by steam, but despite these setbacks he managed to build a reputation as a skilled engine mechanic and to save enough cash to provide Robert with a proper education. In 1814 his first locomotive was built for Killingworth Colliery, and in the next year he devised several methods of increasing its power output.

Robert, meanwhile, had been to school in Newcastle, apprenticed in the colliery business, and later, was even able to afford six months at Edinburgh University. He had worked closely with his father on refining the Killingworth locomotive and had shared with him the education he was receiving. George was appointed as Engineer on the Stockton and Darlington Railway in 1821, and father and son worked together on surveying the route. They designed the engines and organized the factory to build them. George was also responsible for his first iron railway bridge on this line. This was the Gaunless Bridge with four little spans of wrought iron 'lenticular' girders. The top chord acted in compression, like an arch, the ends being kept in by the bottom chord in tension. Each unit thus acted like a beam or girder.

The success of the line led to the appointment of Stephenson Senior as Engineer to the Liverpool and Manchester Railway. This was a huge enterprise for the time—involving a two mile cutting through solid rock at Olive Mount, four miles of problems over the boggy Chat Moss, and no less than 63 bridges in the lines's 30 miles. The biggest bridging project was the construction of the Sankey Viaduct. All the bridges on this route used established techniques in stone and timber. Although, in time, many of the smaller spans were replaced by iron beams, it was only on the later lines, like the London to Birmingham, that iron was used extensively for original bridge work.

The Stephensons' leadership in railway construction was clinched when their locomotive

'Rocket' beat several rival locomotives in 1829 at the Rainhill Trials, organized by the Liverpool and Manchester Company to choose the best one for their new line. Thereafter George was gradually eclipsed by Robert, then 27, who began to take over the railway work.

During the next 30 years, an estimated 9000 miles of railways were laid in Britain, and perhaps some 25,000 railway bridges were put up. Robert Stephenson was responsible for many routes, beginning with the Canterbury and Whitstable and going on to the London and Birmingham (a route he is said to have walked twenty times), and including much of the line from London to Edinburgh.

Socially and economically, the railways had a tremendous impact on patterns of working, manufacturing and marketing. The effects on the landscape were also marked, although they were not always welcomed. When a line was constructed through the beautiful Monsal Dale in Derbyshire, Ruskin complained at the railers, *You enterprised a railway through the valley—you blasted its rocks away. The valley is gone and the gods with it and now every fool in Buxton can be in Bakewell in half an hour and every fool in Bakewell at Buxton; which you think a lucrative exchange—you fools everywhere.* By and large, however, the great railway bridges were acclaimed and admired; two of Stephenson's bridges particularly—the High Level Bridge at Newcastle and the Britannia Bridge over the Menai Straits.

To cross the Tyne at Newcastle, the London to Edinburgh railway had to be carried 130 feet above the river between the high banks some 4000 feet apart. Simple girders of the time were not capable of large enough spans—while a suspension bridge would not have been rigid enough. What Stephenson devised was a series of iron 'bowstring' girders—a form of truss consisting of a cast iron arch rib with the outward thrust taken up, not by the piers, but by a 'bowstring' of wrought iron chains between the ends of each rib. Each span was thus independent and simply rested on each pier. What amazed the public was not this sophisticated principle but the fact that, above the arch was a deck for carrying the railway, and below, a suspended deck for ordinary road traffic. In 1849, the year it was opened, Queen Victoria had stopped her train on the bridge, to admire the structure and gaze at the bustle of Tyneside life far below.

The contractors building the bridge were able to take advantage of improvements being made in all areas of technology. Steam pumps for draining coffer dams, had become much bigger and more efficient. Even more useful was 'Nasmyth's Titanic Steam Hammer', used for driving the foundation piles. This machine astounded onlookers from its

Left above *Causey Arch in County Durham was built in 1721 to carry a colliery tram-way 90 feet over a steep valley. Horse-drawn tram-ways were the precursors of the railways and many eighteenth century mines and iron works had some sort of tram system.*

Left below *George Stephenson's first iron railway span was the Gaunless Bridge at West Auckland, built in 1824 for the Stockton and Darlington Line. The four lenticular iron girders were considered very novel.*

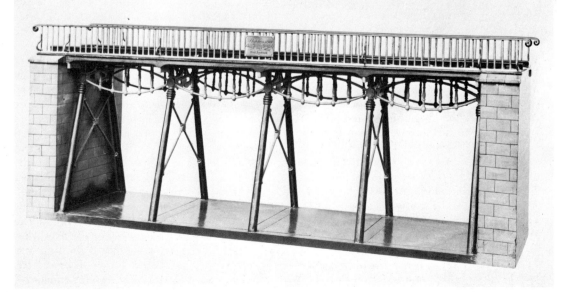

Right *The stone and brick viaduct across the Sankey Canal was the longest bridge on the Liverpool and Manchester Railway. Opened in 1830, the line was the first on which steam locomotives hauled trains for both freight and passengers.*

Right *The 28 arches of Robert Stephenson's Royal Border Bridge across the Tweed at Berwick completed the line from London to Edinburgh. It was opened in 1850 by Queen Victoria.*

Right *The viaduct over the River Wye in Monsal Dale, Derbyshire, was part of the line Ruskin complained about so bitterly. Now disused, the bridge fits more naturally into the landscape.*

first day when it drove the first pile 32 feet into the river bed in four minutes. Further, the use of natural cement was developing again, although the technique of actually manufacturing it was in its infancy. Stephenson was thus able to use concrete in the foundations for the central river pier when quicksands continually flooding the coffer dam made all other solutions impossible.

At the same time as the High Level Bridge was being constructed, Robert Stephenson was also concerned with another difficult crossing. In 1845 he had been appointed as Engineer-in-Chief to the Chester and Holyhead Railway, and was faced with the same problem that Telford had confronted some 25 years before—the Menai Straits. Again the Admiralty specified a lofty clearance, a wide channel and no restrictions to navigation during construction. This time, however, suspension bridges were ruled out as not being stable enough—Captain Brown had constructed a chain bridge used by the Stockton and Darlington Railway in 1830 which had had a very short life. Stephenson devised a bridge formed of two parallel rectangular tubes through which the trains would run. Although the engineers, Thompson and Vignoles, had both designed related structures in the 1840s, it is Robert Stephenson who is popularly held to have proposed the ancestor of the modern box girder. Originally, the tubes were planned to be partly self-supporting, with some of their weight taken by suspension chains. The supporting towers, in fact, were built to accommodate these projected chains.

In designing the bridge, Stephenson adopted what is now common practice—a group approach of collaboration between a number of specialists. William Fairbairn (1789-1874) a practising engineer, made practical tests with special machines on the iron to be used, and built scale models of the various possible tube sections. Professor Eaton Hodgkinson (1789-1861) was a mathematician who had studied the sophisticated French theories and structural formulae. Between them, they established that the compression surfaces of a uniform tube (the roof and upper walls) would fail before the tension surfaces (the floor and lower walls), hence the compression sections had to be thicker than those parts in tension. Fairbairn also found that failure could occur through wrinkling of the side walls, and so recommended using stiffening battens. Their tests and computations established beyond doubt that the tubes could be constructed strongly enough to do without the chains of the original plan.

Work began in April 1846 and proceeded for four years. A work force of some 1500 men, living in a camp on the shore, founded the piers, the central one on the Britannia Rock in midstream, and began the construction of the two shorter shore tubes *in situ*—on wooden staging. The massive 460 foot main spans, however, were built on shore, to be floated out on pontoons between the towers and then lifted into their final positions. Stephenson had a chance to test this method in 1848, when he raised the 412 foot box spans of the Conway Bridge some 18 feet from the water's surface, a complete success. The main Britannia tubes were not so easy. As the tide was floating

Below Robert Stephenson's High Level Bridge, Newcastle, over the River Tyne, was opened in 1849. Trains run on the top deck and road vehicles and footways use the lower deck. Each span has four iron bowstring girders.

Above *The second main span tube of the Britannia Bridge was floated out in December 1844 causing only temporary obstruction to navigation.*

Centre *Robert Stephenson's Britannia Tubular Steel Bridge over the Menai Straits was opened in 1850. The towers were originally built high enough to take suspension chains which eventually proved to be unnecessary. Its 1511 foot overall length made it the world's longest railway bridge until Roebling's Niagara Bridge was opened in 1855.*

Below *One of the four 460 foot long wrought iron tubes for the main spans of the Britannia Bridge which were constructed on shore.*

the first enormous tube towards the Anglesey tower, one of the ropes intended for checking the drifting section at its correct position, jammed on its capstan, and uprooted it. Only by rapidly organizing some of the hundreds of sightseers to hang on to the rope was the capstan foreman able to prevent the box section from missing its mark and drifting away altogether.

Another accident occurred during the lifting operation. The younger engineers assisting Stephenson maintained the tubes could be lifted quickly straight on to their piers. Stephenson, however, insisted that masonry blocks should be laid under each end as the lift proceeded inch by inch. His caution paid off when one of the hydraulic jacks gave way and the tube, weighing some 1600 tons, dropped nine inches on to the packing. Though the damage cost £5000 to put right, the tube had been saved from dropping to the bottom of the Straits.

When, finally, all eight individual tubes were in position, the ends at the approaches were slightly raised, each line of four tubes was rivetted together and the ends lowered. This induced extra stress in the bridge to counteract the natural sagging tendency in the middle of each span. Each tube also became a continuous girder. Along with the box section and the stressing, this is another idea fundamental to bridge building today. A continuous structure is stronger than a number of separate girders, since each span will act with a cantilever effect on the neighbouring spans, and thus provide extra support.

In March 1850 the Britannia Bridge was opened when Robert Stephenson put in the last rivet and walked through one tube, followed by three train loads of revellers. Though the bridge remained the longest rail span in the world for only five years, its design is still an inspiration and example to engineers.

George Stephenson died in 1848 and did not survive to see the completion of his son's bridge—Robert outlived him by only 11 years. He died aged 56, having become the first engineering millionaire and was buried in the Abbey next to Thomas Telford.

Isambard Kingdom Brunel (1806-1859)

The same year saw the death of another great engineering genius of the nineteenth century. In his 53 years Brunel had achieved a monumental amount of tunnelling, building docks, laying out the Great Western Railway, designing three advanced steamships, and, of course, in building several novel bridges. Unlike some of the other great engineers, Brunel had enjoyed a comfortable home background and a good education in England and France. He was sponsored by his father, Marc Brunel, a distinguished engineer in

Above *Stephenson tested the hydraulic jacking system for the Britannia Bridge in 1848 by raising the 412 foot span of the Conway Bridge 18 feet into position. Next to Telford's suspension bridge and in the shadow of Conway castle, Stephenson's structure also sports castellated towers.*

Right Isambard Kingdom Brunel, monomaniac and genius, designed railways, ships and bridges of startling originality but was dogged by ill-fortune.

his own right. Isambard's first job at 18 was assisting Marc in digging the Thames Tunnel between Rotherhithe and Wapping. The work, which lasted several years, was dogged by misfortune and eventually had to be abandoned after two serious floodings. Badly injured in the second of these, Brunel was constrained to spend time convalescing in Bristol from 1829. Here, as we have seen, he conceived and designed the Clifton Suspension Bridge. Despite his success in the design competition he endured several years of frustration trying to establish his professional reputation. Work on the bridge was delayed by civil disturbances over the Great Reform Bill and shortage of money.

However, his work in Bristol had brought him into contact with a group of local businessmen who were planning a Railway Company to build a line from London to Bristol. In 1833, when Brunel was 27, he was appointed engineer to the Company and work began on the Great Western Railway. The first attempt to get an Act through Parliament to allow the Railway to proceed was defeated by rival canal and railway interests in 1834. The next year another bill was presented and Brunel himself was grilled for 11 days by the Parliamentary Committee. With Brunel's impressive evidence and the support of other engineers—Stephenson, Vignoles, Locke and Palmer—the Bill was passed and 'the finest work in England' began.

By 1841 the London-Bristol line was complete and this main line immediately sprouted branches to Oxford and Cheltenham; in all some several hundred miles of railway. The Great Western Railway was faster and more comfortable than

anything in Britain since it used a 7 foot gauge track rather than the 4 foot 8½ inch gauge of the Stephensons' and other northern lines. Brunel's routes required hundreds of bridges, many of which he designed himself with his characteristic originality and lack of regard for convention.

He built, for example, two of the longest, flattest brick arches in the world to carry the Great Western Railway over the Thames at Maidenhead. Each span is 128 feet with a rise of only 24 feet and contemporary observers predicted immediate failure. In fact the eastern arch did sag badly as the centerings first came down, but the builder admitted to being at fault for removing the frame before the Roman cement had properly set. When the main line was quadrupled in 1890-1892, Brunel's plan for the original arches was followed exactly for the extensions and the bridge is still in service.

For railway companies in Devon and Cornwall, Brunel designed a number of standardized wooden viaducts which were easy to construct and maintain. One of the continual problems in the south and west of England was the shortage of skilled construction workers, who tended to be concentrated in the Midlands and North East, where the railways had begun. There are thus interesting comparisons between Brunel's wooden trusses and 'fan' viaducts of the West Country and the structures of the earliest rail-bridge constructors of the United States who often resorted to the standardized patent truss designs which could be put up by virtually any competent carpenter.

Iron, however, was more Brunel's forte, and his two most interesting bridges were iron trusses of an original kind. In 1852 the Chepstow Bridge across the River Wye was opened. The two parallel main spans of 300 feet each consisted of a nine foot wrought iron tube resting on a masonry arch at the shore end and, near the other bank, iron piers extending 50 feet above the railway deck. From each end of the tubes were slung iron chains to support the central section of the span. The whole thing thus acted like a beam of an 'A' cross-section, with the top tube in compression counteracting the tension of the chains below.

Brunel, among others, had assisted Stephenson in the problem of raising the Conway and Britannia Bridge tubes and had gained valuable experience in observing these operations. He was thus able to build the Chepstow trusses on shore, use the tide to float them out between the towers, and within two days, raise the first of them into position on the piers.

Around this time, Brunel was working on an even grander project—a bridge for the Cornwall Railway Company across the Tamar at Saltash. It presented enormous problems. At high water the river was 70 feet deep, so that pier construction would be difficult and expensive. The river was also 1100 feet wide and any bridge would thus require long spans. Finally, the Admiralty again stipulated a minimum headway of 100 feet. Brunel finally decided on two 465 foot spans so that only one, central deep river-pier need be founded. He also decided that the principle of the spans' construction should be a refinement of his Chepstow design. The top tube was to be arched and most of its outward thrust taken up again by suspension chains. The tube was also to be wider, so that the hangers for the rail platform could be vertical—and the cross section of the truss made rectangular rather than triangular.

After one false start in 1849 when the Company ran out of capital, work was begun in earnest in 1853. For laying the foundations for the deep water pier, Brunel and his engineers developed a technique they had been forced to use for the main piers at Chepstow. There, the sinking of the eight foot diameter foundation pipes into the river bed had been made impossible by water and quick-sand flowing up inside the pipe. The solution had been to cap off the pipe, pump in compressed air and have the workmen inside the pipe excavating away and passing sand and mud out through air locks. For Saltash, Brunel designed a great double cylinder 35 feet wide, with an outer space under compressed air for the workmen to excavate the river bed and an inner chamber, under normal pressure, for the masons to lay the stone foundations once the whole thing had reached hard bedrock.

As the piers were being constructed, the huge girders were taking shape on shore. Ironically, the tension chains used had been purchased from the Clifton Bridge Company who were in financial difficulties. Brunel's earliest and most favourite project was still not progressing smoothly. In September 1857, the first 1000 ton Saltash span was floated out. Brunel himself stood on top of the truss and supervised the whole procedure with a system of semaphore signalling devised for the

Left *Brunel's Chepstow Bridge over the River Wye was opened in 1852. The iron trusses are 50 feet deep and the twin spans 300 feet. The river piers were excavated by workmen inside tubes working under compressed air. The spans were floated out and lifted complete in the same way as those of the Britannia Bridge.*

Left *The most celebrated of Brunel's several brick bridges at Maidenhead over the River Thames. The shallowness of the 128 foot arches led many to predict its collapse, but it is still in use.*

Left above *Such enthusiasm did Queen Victoria's consort have for Brunel's structure that he allowed it to be called the Royal Albert Bridge. Brunel, however, only just lived long enough to see his bridge completed in 1859.*

Left below *Brunel developed his lenticular trusses for the bridge over the Tamar at Saltash from his Chepstow Bridge. It is seen here under construction in 1858 during the raising of the second 465 foot span.*

Right above *Brunel's standardized designs for the Cornwall Railway Company, such as this wooden 'fan' viaduct at Penryn, could be quickly and cheaply erected and easily maintained.*

Right centre *The Crumlin Viaduct, Ebbw Vale, was part of the Newport, Abergavenny and Hereford Railway. Many high iron viaducts like this were constructed in many parts of the world on early lines.*

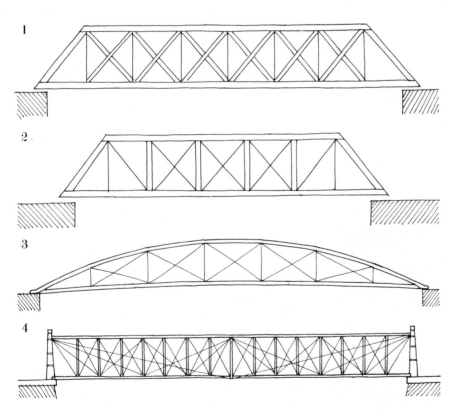

occasion. The festive crowds watched in dead silence until the great span finally came to rest——then the band of the Royal Marines played *Hail the Conquering Hero Comes* and the crowds cheered as Brunel stepped down.

But in May 1859 when Prince Albert finally opened the bridge amid further wild enthusiasm, Brunel was not there. He had worn himself out on his last grand scheme—his third ship, the vast *Great Eastern*. Before his death, however, he was drawn over the completed bridge on a special wagon for a final inspection.

It must not be forgotten that, although the most significant early development of the railways and railway bridge design occurred in England, railways were also being built throughout Europe and the rest of the world. British engineers were much in demand from early days. Thomas Telford himself had been responsible for the Gotha canal in Sweden. Joseph Locke and Charles Blacker Vignoles had both been involved with the Stephensons on the Liverpool and Manchester line, and went on to engineer many lines on their own. Vignoles went on to survey and lay out railroads in Switzerland, Brazil and Spain. Locke progressed from the Grand Junction and London and Southampton lines to build, with his English contractor Brassey and 5000 imported navvies, the Paris to Le Havre Railway in 1847. The most notable event on that line had been the collapse of the twenty-seven 50 foot arches of the Barentin Viaduct, due to undue loading on one of the arches before proper 'settling'. As one arch failed the whole bridge went down from progressive collapse. Within a year Brassey rebuilt it to exactly the same specification at his own expense. It is still standing and in 1950 it was renamed the Joseph Locke Viaduct.

The works of Robert Stephenson were of course widely exported—his 'Planet' locos were used on some of the earliest railroads in the United States, and his 'Patentee' engines pulled the first trains in France, the Netherlands, the German states, Russia and Italy in the 1830s and 1840s. His box girder bridges at Menai and Conway led a North American company to invite him to create a similar but longer structure over the St Lawrence at Montreal. Brunel, too, was in demand overseas. For example, while on holiday away from the strains of building the *Great Eastern*, he was working on plans for the East Bengal Railway.

North America

In North America, bridge building continued to develop in two separate ways. One strand was the gradual evolution of more sophisticated structural and theoretical analyses applied to the wooden truss, combined with the gradual replacement of timber with wrought and cast iron as materials for bridge building. The other strand continued the pragmatic tradition of building in timber as the railways thrust westward as fast as they could.

The first patent truss to incorporate iron into the basically timber fabric was the Howe Truss,

Above *In North America many patent truss designs were developed during the transition from timber, through iron, to steel. (1) William Howe's patent was a timber truss strengthened with vertical iron tension rods; (2)Thomas Pratt reversed this using diagonal tension members. His design became standard in steel trusses; (3) Squire Whipple's bowstring truss was essentially similar in principle to Stephenson's High Level Bridge; (4) Albert Fink's system was one of several refinements of all iron railroad bridges.*

which had top and bottom chords and diagonal bracing in timber, and vertical iron rods in tension. This basic design was used, with modifications, late into the nineteenth century. The first scientifically designed truss was the Pratt patent, which reversed the Howe system and incorporated vertical timber members in compression and diagonal iron rods in tension. The structural principle in this design was used well into the twentieth century when all parts were made in steel. In 1847 one Squire Whipple took design in iron a stage further when he patented an all-iron truss with cast compression members in top chords and vertical supports, and wrought members for the diagonals and lower chords in tension.

Whipple published *A Work on Bridge Design*, the first correct analysis of the stresses in a truss structure, and the application of this type of analysis was developed further by Albert Fink and Wendell Bollman in further patent all-iron designs. Simultaneously other writers, like Carl Culmann (Bavarian), Herman Haupt (American) and Robert Bow (English) reached similar conclusions, and iron girder trusses became widespread. Also, some of the older designs, like the Town Lattice truss, were adapted for use with the new materials.

On some of the long pioneer lines however, iron was harder to come by, so timber trestles were thrown up, as rapidly as possible, often using the forest on either side of the track. The raw materials were thus abundant and the trestle's design so straightforward, it needed little in the way of highly skilled labour to erect. This was an important consideration during the American Civil War, when, for the first time, railways played an important tactical part. Railway bridges became targets for artillery or for sabotage and in some places needed frequent rebuilding.

In most instances in North America, the buildings of the railways was a great political as well as financial undertaking. For example, the speed at which the Canadian Pacific Railroad could be pushed through was crucial, not only to the staggering overdrafts of backers like Donald Smith of the Hudson Bay Company, but also for the political future of the whole province of British Columbia. Without the coast-to-coast railway link, the province would have been annexed by the United States. Time simply could not be spent on designing, testing and building elaborate new bridges.

The failures of iron

Overall, the century from 1780 to 1880 was an age of iron, in increasing quantity and increasingly sophisticated designs. In the 1860s and 1870s in France for example, Gustave Eiffel was designing high iron viaducts for the coal and ore trains over the steep valleys of the Massif Central. He used advanced methods of computing not only loads and bending moments within the structure, but, for the first time, also went into detail on the effects of wind on bridges.

Although the effects of wind had been studied on one or two bridges, such as the Britannia bridge, not all designers had been as careful as Eiffel, and in the last quarter of the century, the

Right *Timber trestles were very important during the American Civil War because they were quick and relatively simple to erect. This photograph by Mathew Brady shows the Northern locomotive 'Fire Fly' on a narrow field bridge.*

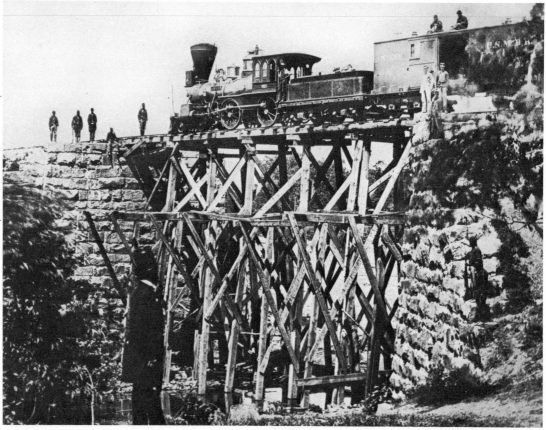

early enthusiasm for iron was reduced by a number of bridge failures, which showed up its basic defects as a structural material. In 1865 the first all-iron Howe truss design had been put up at Ashtabula to carry the Lake Shore Railway over a steep gorge near Lake Erie. On a snowy December night eleven years later, it collapsed under an eleven-car train, carrying 92 people to their deaths in the ravine below. The engine driver of the leading locomotive described later how he watched the train disappearing behind him and managed to save himself by accelerating up the sinking structure. A public and press outcry following the accident drove the railroad's engineer to suicide. It seems, however, that the main reason for failure was a combination of the lack of knowledge about the behaviour of wrought iron under tension, and the fact that the bridge had a high dead-load (or self-weight) and was insufficiently braced. More simply the accident showed that in poor designs, iron was too heavy and unreliable to hold itself up.

Cast iron, of course, was even more unreliable in tension and this was recognized early on. However, Robert Stephenson, in a rail bridge he built over the River Dee, discovered that there were limits even to its strength in compression. His bridge consisted of two parallel cast iron girders, strengthened in their tension zones with wrought iron chain-links. With the straps tightened, ballast laid under the rails, and a train on the bridge, it is thought the top edges of the cast girders (the compression zone), buckled outwards and snapped. Although it is still not agreed how the bridge collapsed, its failure underlines the

difficulties and ignorance in building with these materials.

The other great truss bridge failure was the Tay Bridge disaster of 1879. Though hailed as a masterpiece by Queen Victoria and everyone else, 75 people perished in the Tay when a six-coach passenger train was crossing the central section of 13 'high girders' and both the train and the girders were blown sideways into the Firth. One of the reports of the inquiry into the accident concluded the bridge had been *badly designed, badly constructed and badly maintained*. The designer, Thomas Bouch, had taken no special account of the effects of side winds combined with moving loads. The cast iron pillars and wrought trusses had not been strong enough to stand up to the 70 to 80 miles per hour gale that had been blowing.

During the 1880s iron railway bridges in the United States were failing at a rate of 25 a year. Two things became necessary; first, a new structural material which would behave predictably and work as well in tension as in compression; and secondly, a greater number of specialist civil engineers with particular skills in bridge design, analysis and construction. The emergence of the latter was a gradual process within the civil engineering profession, but from the late 1800s some engineers appeared who are remembered specifically as bridge designers rather than the all-rounders of the profession's early days. Steel, the much needed new material, after a lengthy period of development and experiment with production techniques, however, quickly superseded iron as a structural material.

Below *Rescue boats and divers searched unsuccessfully for survivors of the Tay Bridge disaster. Sir Thomas Bouch, the designer, had not made enough provision for the combined wind resistance of a train in the high girders in the centre of the bridge. Seventy-five people died when a gale blew the 13 spans down as the evening mail to Dundee was crossing on the night of December 28 1879.*

Steel

Previous page Open hearth steel and Sir John Fowler's and Benjamin Baker's cantilever design made this structure over the Firth of Forth one of the world's strongest railway bridges. It was opened in 1890 by the Prince of Wales, and Fowler, Baker and the contractor, William Arrol, received royal honours.

WHEN THE WORLD price of steel dropped by 75 percent in the 1870s, a new phase of bridge building was heralded. The new material was more versatile than any previously used in bridge construction. It enabled all the established bridging methods to reach new peaks of development. Steel also provided its own possibilities of new forms, and enabled concrete, the other new material of the late nineteenth century, to evolve as an effective medium.

Steel bridges have been built for about a hundred years, in which time there has been a vast growth in urban populations, in industrial production and in science and technology. The period has also seen the gradual change in emphasis in bulk transport systems, from rail to road. These changes have all contributed to the erection of a vast number of steel bridges of many different structural types. It thus becomes very complicated to follow the history of bridge building through in strict chronological order. What must be done, therefore, is to look at the main types of bridges which use steel and deal with them in sections.

Chronologically, however, we can distinguish three loose 'periods' in steel bridge making. When thinking about the development of one type of steel bridge, it is important to bear in mind that other types were developing at the same time, and that before any bridge was put up, very serious thought had to be given to the question of the most suitable alternative form for the particular crossing.

The first phase of bridges in steel was a 'pioneer' phase between the 1870s and the early years of the twentieth century. Towards the end of that period, steel became established as clearly preferable to iron, as cantilevers, trusses and arches were built on a scale undreamed of before. Most of the big bridges of the time were for rail transport and thus had to be both extremely strong and resistant to damage from vibration.

The second phase was between the beginning of the twentieth century and the early thirties. First in the United States, and then in Europe, the internal combustion engine began to make its presence felt. After some very massive railway bridges in the 1910s and 1920s, bridges began to appear specifically for motor vehicles. During this second phase, came a refinement of technique in the use of steel and a move towards lighter and more economical structures.

This move gradually evolved into the third phase covering the last thirty years or so, where road bridges became the most usual type of long span, and the suspension bridge the most spectacularly successful form of long road-bridge construction. However, although the longest spans nowadays attract the most public attention, it must not be forgotten that the construction of road links, for example, with modern motorways, very often depends more on the construction of short and medium span erections to eliminate gradients, than upon great individual bridges across unique obstructions. This last phase includes, therefore, both the tremendously long road bridge spans and

Above *Captain James
Eads used steel for the
tubular ribs and couplings
in the bridge to carry road
and rail across the
Mississippi at St Louis.
It was opened in 1874 and
is still safely carrying
heavier loads than it was
originally designed for.*

able to exploit the uneven quality of early steel and to continue to win contracts for their pre-fabricated iron designs. By the 1880s, however, quality control of steel production was possible, and steel showed as clearly preferable to iron. For any given weight, a piece of steel was stronger than either cast or wrought iron. It was strong in compression and in tension. It was ductile rather than brittle, and could be rolled, cast or drawn into many different shapes—blocks, tubes, girders or wires.

The very first bridge to have incorporated steel in its fabric was a 334 foot suspension span over the Danube Canal at Vienna, designed by Ignaz Edlen von Mitis and opened as early as 1828. Steel was used for the eyebars. When steel prices dropped in the 70s and 80s, however, the first important bridges to use steel were constructed in the United States. The Eads Bridge (1874), across the Mississippi at St Louis had steel arches; the Glasgow Bridge (1878) over the Missouri consisted of five Whipple steel trusses; and the Brooklyn New York (1883) was a steel wire-cable suspension bridge. Here we will concentrate on arches, trusses and cantilevers. Suspension bridges have a history of their own and are treated separately in the next chapter.

Arches

In the middle of the nineteenth century, St Louis was the most important centre in the American Mid-West. Situated near the confluence of the Missouri and Mississippi rivers, it had grown up both as a focus of north-south river traffic and of east-west overland routes. With the coming of the railroads however, its development was threatened by the rapid growth of Chicago. In 1850, the citizens of St Louis realized that the Mississippi, over a quarter of a mile wide, had to be bridged, and for some 15 years a number of proposals had been drawn up by the most eminent bridge designers of the day but all were rejected. All the plans proposed foundations on piles, and none of them took enough notice of the particularly treacherous nature of the river bed. The sand and mud of the bottom was liable to change level drastically from season to season with the huge variations in the volume of water (and of ice in the winter) coming down the river.

The design that was eventually accepted in 1866 did not come from a bridge engineer, but from an extraordinary character named Captain James Buchanan Eads, who had spent his life on the river as, among other things, steamboat engineer, salvage operator and designer and builder of ironclad gunboats during the Civil War. He thus knew the river intimately and had the trust and respect of the City Fathers of St Louis. His proposal was for three 500 foot arches in steel supported on two piers and end abutments whose foundations should rest on the solid rock below the mud and sand of the river bed.

Captain Eads had very few precedents to guide him through the six years of construction. He had

the more humdrum developments in steel bridges which make modern motor transport systems feasible.

Steel is really no more than very highly refined iron, with a carefully controlled low carbon content. Different techniques of making steel had been known in China (about 200 BC), India (about 500 AD) and in medieval Europe and Japan. But all the techniques were slow, laborious processes requiring a great deal of time and energy to produce minute amounts. Steel was thus so expensive that before the late nineteenth century its use was limited to edged tools and weapons. During the Crimean War (1854-56) an Englishman, Henry Bessemer, was developing a technique for bulk steel production for gun barrels. The Bessemer Converter was invented in 1856, and, although it did not work perfectly at first, the technique of blowing air through molten iron to burn off impurities became the first practicable method of bulk steel production. It was followed in 1867 by the success of what became known as the Siemans-Martins open hearth method, evolved in Birmingham, England by the German-born Charles William Siemans and the French iron-makers Pierre and Emile Martins.

The first steel bridges

In the early days of steel, there was stiff competition from the bridge companies producing their patent iron structures, particularly in America. Organizations like the old Keystone, Phoenix and Baltimore Bridge companies were

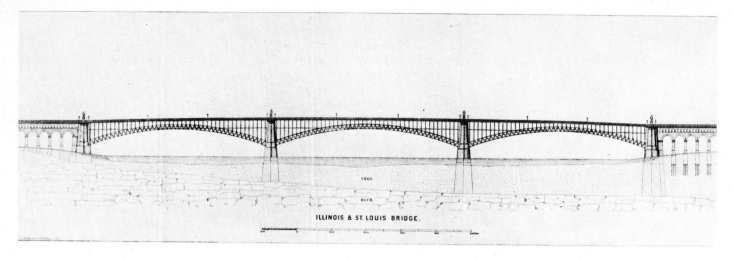

ILLINOIS & ST. LOUIS BRIDGE.

to cope not only with the technical problems of founding the piers at enormous depths and building arches in a new material, but also with a great number of human problems created by rival bridge companies and doubtful, conservative engineers. There were also a number of financial crises, for as the work progressed it became clear that the bridge would cost twice as much as originally planned. Eads himself dealt with this whole range of difficulties and became ill several times for his efforts. He had complete confidence in his plans, and managed to scotch all criticisms in his vigorous reports to the St Louis and Illinois Bridge Company. Answering the objections of Henry Linville, a distinguished consulting engineer who believed that Eads' unprecedented arches would collapse, he wrote:

Must we admit that because a thing has never been done it can never be, when our knowledge and judgement assures us that it is entirely practicable?

The decision to use steel for the arches of the Eads' bridge was one of the several major applications of building techniques then in their infancy. The other principal developments were in the use of pneumatic caissons for the foundations at a tremendous depth, and the technique of constructing the arches without centering. This was achieved by cantilevering the arch sections out towards each other, supported on cables stretched from temporary towers. The huge pneumatic caissons, designed by Eads, were floated into position and as they were dug into the river bed, the masonry was laid in the caisson. When they reached rock, the shafts and working spaces were filled with concrete.

Because of the great depth of the foundations, the pressure of air inside the caissons had to be high enough to keep the water and mud out while digging went on. The main problem of working at such pressure was that many of the workmen developed 'caisson disease'. It is now known that this is due to the build-up of nitrogen in the bloodstream during too rapid decompression— 'the bends' of deep-sea diving. Some 15 St Louis workmen died and many others suffered more or less serious paralysis, before Eads' own family physician established a work, rest and diet routine and a rule for slow decompression,

which finally managed to contain the problem. The east abutment was the last foundation to be laid, and although by far the deepest—136 feet below high water, there was only one fatal accident and that was from a flagrant breech of rules.

Eads' other achievement was to ensure the quality of the steel tubes for the arch-ribs, by drawing up very high technical specifications for the parts and devising a machine for testing every one. Several of his suppliers, like the Butcher Steel Works, were driven to the verge of bankruptcy by the exacting standards. Andrew Carnegie (who built his reputation on his fabricating and financing work on the St Louis Bridge) was contracted for much of the steel and had to ensure supplies 'even if it cost as much as silver'. Although Eads' standards meant delays when parts could not be accepted, they did ensure the continuing strength of the St Louis Bridge. They also forced the development of higher standards of steel making generally.

Associated with Eads on this great project were a number of able engineers who bore the brunt of the actual detailed design and construction work; men like Colonel Henry Flad, Charles Pfieffer, Charles Shaler Smith and Theodore Cooper who were to go on to distinguished bridge building careers of their own. Henry Linville, a famous designer of truss bridges who had earlier mistrusted Eads' plan, was persuaded to join the project by his partner in the Keystone Bridge Company, Andrew Carnegie.

The St Louis Bridge, the combined efforts of these men, was opened with a huge city-wide celebration on July 4 1874. President Grant was there, steam-boat men massed their hooting craft below the bridge, there were speeches, processions and the most spectacular firework display anyone could remember. In his book *Bridges: The Spans of North America* David Plowden says *While most other bridges of that vintage have long since been replaced, including all of Linville's, the Eads continues to carry the same heavy traffic as it did in 1874.* This is itself an understatement since loads today are far heavier than in Eads' own time.

In France, the spread of the railways and the growth of industry were somewhat slower than in Britain or the United States. To some extent, this

Above *Elevation of the Eads' bridge showing the shallow segmental profile of the arches and the tremendous depth of foundations necessary to find bedrock. The arches were cantilevered out from temporary towers at the piers and abutments.*

was associated with the shortage and inaccessibility of raw materials. Many important mineral deposits were located in the high, inhospitable plains of the Massif Central and exploitation of the mining products depended on the construction of railway links to the large towns of Lyons and Limoges. In 1879, Alexandre Gustave Eiffel (1832-1923) had been working on some of these difficult lines for some 15 years. He had been constructing many fine iron viaducts across the steep gorges of the area, and he had evolved sophisticated methods of designing iron pylons and truss decks to stand up to the high winds which were funnelled down the valleys. In his early work, he had even designed and set up several sophisticated meteorological stations to study the problems.

Eiffel was consulted by a group of government engineers planning a new and difficult link from the southern Massif Central to the main Paris-Lyons-Marseilles line. He proposed that one particularly roundabout route could be avoided by a 400 foot high viaduct over the River Truyère. Since Eiffel was the only man capable of designing such a structure, in June 1879, the Ministry gave him the job. The Garabit viaduct, Eiffel's solution to the Truyère crossing, highlights the nature of the changeover from iron to steel. Difficulties in manufacture meant that in the 1880s, steel was by no means established as the better material. Thus Eiffel preferred iron for his great parabolic arch of 530 feet. The cross section of the trusswork of the Garabit arch is ingenious. At the crown of the arch, the truss is narrow and deep to support the deck truss carrying the railway. Towards the abutments the section becomes wider and shallower, to counteract the overturning effects of the side winds. The ends of the arch rest on hinges which allow for expansion and contraction of the steel with changes in weather conditions. This 'two-hinged' concept is one that subsequently became almost standard for great steel arches and is particularly well demonstrated in the Tyne Bridge in Newcastle. The other aspect of both Eiffel's Garabit Viaduct and Eads' St Louis Bridge that became standard was the cantilever method of construction—as arch spans became longer and higher the feasibility of erecting supporting falsework decreased.

Another early steel arch of note was the Victoria Falls Bridge, completed in 1907, which links the borders of Rhodesia and Zambia, then Southern and Northern Rhodesia. Although the link was originally conceived by Cecil Rhodes as part of his great imperialist scheme for a railway across Africa from Cape to Cairo, the actual construction had to wait until the bridge building technology of steel caught up with the idea.

Again, the Victoria Falls Bridge was a deck

Below *The Garabit viaduct, designed by Gustave Eiffel, was opened in 1884. Although built in wrought iron, the two-hinged crescent arch predicted steel structural shapes. Tests showed that a 400 ton train in the centre of the 530 foot arch, 480 feet above the River Truyère, deflected the structure one third of an inch.*

arch structure, but in 1916 the first great 'through arch' appeared. This was Gustav Lindenthal's Hell Gate Bridge spanning 1000 feet over the East River in New York, and set a new standard for steel arches. In a through arch, the deck intersects the line of the arch so that the central part of the deck is suspended from the arch above, while the ends are supported from below where the arch approaches the abutments. Earlier bridges to use this format had included the Niagara, Clifton bridge (840 feet) and a bridge at Düsseldorf (595 feet) both in 1898, and the Bellows Falls bridge (540 feet) of 1905. The East River was Lindenthal's most difficult problem in making the much needed direct railroad connection between Pennsylvania to the west of New York, and Long Island to the east. He made several proposals for the bridge including plans for trusses, a cantilever and a two-hinged crescent arch like Eiffel's Garabit Viaduct.

The plan which was accepted and built was, at the time, awesome in its scale and, although its span was later overtaken by the Sydney Harbour and Bayonne Bridges in Australia and the United States, it remains an outstanding example of the

monumental age of building in steel.

While in these arches, the whole integrated structure contributes towards carrying the total load, ultimately, the load is focussed on the abutments via the end members of the bottom chord. The bridge is thus a two-hinged arch with the deck suspended from the arch. Over 80,000 tons of steel went into the construction of the Hell Gate bridge and its approaches. The builders faced severe problems in moving the largest pieces—the four lower chord end sections, 185 tons each—on to the site.

The greatest problem however, had cropped up in laying foundations. Under one of the abutment positions a large fault in the bedrock was discovered too late to alter the site. Half a million dollars had to be spent on creating a huge concrete bridge over the fault to form an adequate foundation. All the dangerous work had to be carried out from pneumatic caissons 70 feet below river level.

The two halves of the arch were cantilevered out from each side over the furious tides of the East River. Each rib was supported during erection by large cables passed back to shore anchorages over 2500 ton hydraulic jacks. When the ribs were complete, each jack was lowered to bring the ends together. It is a measure of the increasing accuracy in engineering practice that the amount of lowering necessary for this operation agreed with the calculated prediction to within 1/32 of an inch.

The handsome architectural style of the Hell Gate arch is thought to have been important in the original decision to build an arch rather than a cantilever. In the early 1920s the city of Sydney was considering a similar range of proposals for a monumental bridge between the northern and southern halves of the city. Dr John Bradfield, Chief Engineer of the New South Wales Government, had studied many of the world's long-span bridges, and on the basis of the Hell Gate Bridge, had drawn up a general plan very similar. Although many other proposals were submitted, Sydney chose a plan very close to Bradfield's outline, put in by the English firm of Dorman Long and Company. The chief designer was Ralph Freeman who was the consulting engineer of Sir Douglas Fox and Partners of London.

The bridge was to be a symbol of Australia's industrial maturity—the world's longest steel span over one of the world's finest natural harbours. By any standards, the undertaking was massive and, even now, Sydney Harbour Bridge still holds the world record for heaviest load. It now carries eight lanes of road traffic, four railway tracks for both main line and suburban trains, and two footpaths.

Although during the seven years of construction, strikes and labour problems caused many delays, the building of the bridge was very much an Australian achievement. One third of the steel in the bridge was Australian, the ribs and panel sections were fabricated by Australian labour in the large workshops on the north shore. All the stone for the towers came from a specially opened granite quarry some 200 miles from Sydney.

The arch was built again by cantilevering each half out from the shore, with additional support from 128 large anchoring cables on each side. The cables were later used in the Indooroopily suspension bridge near Brisbane. The parts for the arch were hoisted into position from barges by a large travelling crane on each arm. Each crane weighed 565 tons and had a lifting capacity of 120 tons.

Below The design of high viaducts in steel owed much to Eiffel's work on the effects of wind on high structures. Lethbridge Viaduct carries the Canadian Pacific Railroad 5327 feet across the valley of Old Man River in Alberta. It was completed in 1909.

Left above *Some 37,000 tons of steel went into the arch of the Sydney Harbour Bridge, designed by Sir Ralph Freeman. Special steel fences had to be erected to stop suicides leaping into the harbour.*

Left below *The Sydney Harbour Bridge in New South Wales was built between 1925 and 1932 to carry road and rail links crucial to the development of the city. The two hinged arch has a 1650 foot clear span.*

Right below *The two halves of the Sydney Harbour Bridge approaching at mid-span. To take some of the enormous weight of each cantilevered arm, plus travelling cranes, cables were anchored back from the top chords until the arch was complete.*

Above *The Bayonne Bridge, carrying a toll road over the Kill van Kull in New York, was opened four months before the Sydney Harbour Bridge, with a span just 25 inches longer. The abutment towers were originally to have been encased in concrete.*

The loading on each arm as it approached meeting point was thus enormous, and the joining of the arch in August 1930 was an extremely tricky operation. Once the arch was closed, the hangers and deck were suspended. The whole structure was tested by loading the four railway tracks on the arch with 72 locomotives weighing a total of 7600 tons.

When the bridge was opened on March 19 1932, however, the celebrations were marred by the fact that four months earlier in New York, a steel arch bridge had been opened which was 25 *inches* longer. The Bayonne Bridge over the Kill van Kull had a span of 1652 feet to Sydney's 1650 feet, and had been constructed in just two years. It has been established that the design for the span of the American bridge was a deliberate attempt to gain a world record. The Bayonne Bridge, however, is a highway toll bridge and so carries much lighter loads than Sydney Harbour, and is visually and architecturally less satisfying.

Although, in these bridges, it is the hinges of the bottom chord at the abutments which take the main thrust, the top chord and the trusswork

Below The versatility of steel has been used to create arches of different types: (1) fixed-end deck arch, with the roadway supported wholly from below; (2) two-hinged through arch supporting the roadway both from below and overhead; (3) tied arch, similar in action to a simple girder; (4) the combination trussed arch.

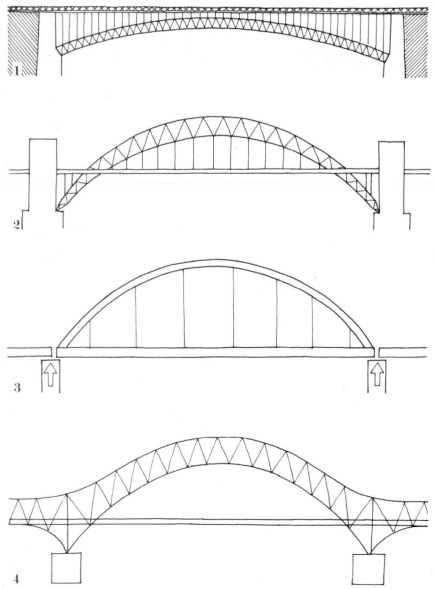

makes them look like fixed-end arches. Therefore, visually, these bridges need a heavy abutment to make them look stable. The Hell Gate and Sydney Harbour Bridges have stone end towers to create this effect. The Bayonne Bridge, however, does not. Since the towers are not necessary for the function of the bridge, the Port of New York Authority decided not to clad the steel end-towers in concrete, in order to save money. The Bayonne Bridge, therefore, looks curiously unfinished, with the metal towers at the abutments apparently too light to contain the thrust of the arch.

These two bridges of the early thirties indicate the growing impact of road transport, and the fact that, after that time, fewer and fewer great bridge structures were created for railways. Although steel arches were originally developed for railways, their use has continued well into the automobile era. This is partly due to the fact that the arch form can be used in such a variety of ways, and that wherever used, an arch has a kind of intrinsic dramatic appeal lacking in some other forms.

In addition to the types already mentioned, are the tied arch and the continuous trussed arch. A tied arch should be properly considered as a type of girder, since the outward thrust at the arch ends is not taken on abutments or foundations. As with Robert Stephenson's High Level Bridge at Newcastle, the thrust is taken by 'bowstring' girders in tension between the ends of the arch although, of course, steel had made possible much longer spans than Stephenson's. This technique has been used many times for

medium spans, two examples being the Chesapeake City Bridge over the Chesapeake and Delaware Canal in Maryland in the United States, and the Scotswood Bridge at Blaydon in England.

Finally, the hybrid form of a combination of the truss and arch enables the bridge designer to combine the approach span trusses with the main span arch in a continuous unified structure, rather than using separate techniques for each. How such bridges 'work' is rather complicated to analyze since they include the characteristics of a fixed-end arch as well as those of cantilevers. This is a fairly rare type, although one good example is the Runcorn-Widnes Road Bridge across the River Mersey. It was constructed, like the Sydney Harbour Bridge, by Dorman Long and Company and opened in 1961.

Cantilevers

Arch bridges had been constructed for centuries in every other material before steel became available. However, it was not until the advent of steel that the cantilever principle became really feasible as a form for long spans. Again it was the railways that provided the first great stimulus for this kind of bridge. The first spectacular success for the cantilever form was the Firth of Forth Railway Bridge. When it was completed in 1890, its size and design were unprecedented. What is more remarkable is that it has remained in service for 85 years, and is the second longest cantilever span in the world.

The Firth of Forth was a serious obstacle to travel from Edinburgh to Perth, Dundee and

Aberdeen. Proposals to replace the three ferry services with a bridge had been made as early as 1818 when a totally impracticable suspension bridge had been proposed by an Edinburgh civil engineer named James Anderson. The North British Railway Company suggested a 500 foot span in 1860, but their scheme was not implemented. In 1873 the Forth Bridge Company was founded and a design for a suspension bridge was submitted by Sir Thomas Bouch. The plan was accepted and work eventually began. In 1879 Bouch's Tay Bridge was blown down. Doubts about his designing abilities, combined with general doubts about suspension spans for railways, persuaded the Company to stop work on the project.

At the time, cantilever bridges were in their infancy. The earliest modern form had been constructed in Hassfurt over the River Main in Germany by Heinrich Gerber, with a central span of 124 feet. In the United States, Charles Shaler Smith had built the Kentucky River Viaduct (three 375 feet spans) in 1876, and C. H. Parker had put up several shorter 'iron truss cantilevers' anchored by tension rods. For some years, Benjamin Baker, a member of Sir John Fowler's engineering office in London, had been advocating cantilevers for long spans, in articles and lectures. In 1881, Baker and Fowler submitted a new plan for the Forth Railway Bridge and, on the strength of their proposals, were made engineers-in-chief.

Both men were already distinguished engineers. Sir John Fowler had served as engineer to the Stockton and Darlington Railway and had also

Above *The Runcorn-Widnes Bridge on opening day in July 1961. The refined steel arch provided a badly needed road link across the River Mersey to replace the old transporter bridge seen in the background.*

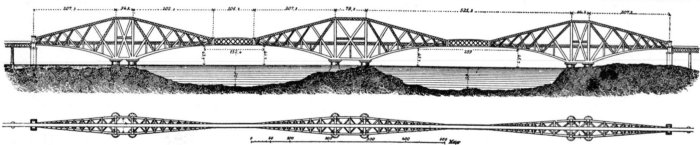

developed many lines in the east of England. In London, he had been responsible for much of the city's local railway system. He had also worked in Egypt on railway systems, factories and irrigation projects, which had earned him a knighthood. In 1865 Fowler was elected as the President of the Institute of Civil Engineers. His younger partner, Benjamin Baker, was known as an authority on bridge design and had worked on the London Metropolitan Line. (He had also designed the cylindrical canister in which Cleopatra's Needle was shipped to England.)

Strenuous opposition was marshalled against their enormous proposal. Rival railway companies enlisted the help of doubting engineers and of the ferry interests of the Firth, but the Bill for the Bridge was passed in 1882 and work began shortly afterwards. First came the digging of the 12 foundations for the three towers. Two factors helped the use of pneumatic caissons. First,

suitable rock was not very deep, and second, the fire hazards of working in compressed air had been greatly reduced by the invention of electric lamps.

After the masonry courses had been laid in the concrete-sealed caissons, the three huge steel towers were begun. When they were complete, the cantilever arms were built out towards each other, symmetrically to keep the stresses even within the structure. All the steelwork was cut and shaped in what was, essentially, a small industrial town built specially for the project to house the army of up to 4000 workers. The contractors, headed by William Arrol, organized a fleet of steam boats for transporting steel parts out to the growing bridge. Rescue boats were also continually on duty round each cantilever (for the record, they saved eight lives and retrieved some 8000 caps and other articles of clothing).

The two suspended spans, linking the ends of the cantilever arms, were themselves cantilevered out 151 feet above the water. The final joining up of these spans was one of the most delicate parts of the whole operation. The final design called for one end of each suspended span to be free to move to take up expansion and contraction in the steel fabric. To build the spans out, however, both ends needed to be fixed temporarily to the main cantilever. To make the suspended spans functional, therefore, needed first a steadily high temperature to expand the steel fabric so both the bottom chords of the suspended truss could be joined; then a slight fall in temperature to shrink the bridge and deflect the top chords downwards so they could be joined; finally another rise in temperature to take the strain off the temporarily fixed ends of the suspended spans, so the securing bolts could be removed and the bridge left to expand and contract without setting up undue stresses.

What was needed, in fact, was one day of reasonable weather followed by a cool night and then another reasonable day. However, this perfectly normal sequence of events did not occur for either span, and fires had to be lit under various members to produce the right effects. In October 1889 one bottom chord only of the first suspended span could be fixed before nightfall and an anxious night was spent hoping the temperature would not fall to widen the gap between the other bottom chord ends. Luckily it did not and the gap was closed next day. By November 14, the second span had been joined but the temporary fixing bolts not yet removed, when it seems there was a sudden drop in temperature. The fixing bolts sheared with a sound like a cannon shot and the entire structure trembled. However, the bolts that sheared were those due for removal anyway, and although the event caused consternation to those on the bridge, no harm was done.

Apart from the cantilever/suspended span principles of the Forth Bridge, its most impressive feature is its sheer size. Into the bridge went 58,000 tons of open-hearth steel, and although the effect is spectacular, the bridge has been criticized for being 'unnecessarily' strong. Baker and Fowler were, in fact, extremely cautious on two aspects of their design. First, with the Tay Bridge disaster fresh in the public memory, the effects of side winds had to be catered for. After many experiments, it was decided that the bridge should be able to withstand wind pressures that, by today's standards would be considered unnecessarily high, even in a part of the world subject to gales. Second, since steel was such a relatively new material, the margins the designers allowed themselves were very generous, especially for the parts of the bridge that would be subject to fatigue from the repeated vibration of passing trains.

The bridge was officially opened on March 4 1890, by the Prince of Wales (later King Edward VII) and was seen as a triumph of Victorian engineering and a symbol of Scotland's greatness. Benjamin Baker and William Arrol were knighted, Sir John Fowler received a baronetcy.

One engineer who criticized the bridge for its unnecessary size and weight, and its excessive use of steel, was Theodore Cooper. In 1900, at the peak of a distinguished career, he was taken on as consulting engineer by the Quebec Bridge and Railway Company, to select and approve a design for a great bridge across the St Lawrence River. The Company was under heavy financial pressure to minimize the amount of steel in the bridge. The design selected by Cooper was by P. L. Szlapka and the Phoenix Bridge Company and was 'the cheapest and the best'—a 1600 foot cantilever, superficially akin to the Forth Bridge, but using much lighter members. Cooper's recommendation of an increase in the span to 1800 feet was adopted. By July 1907, work on the south cantilever arm was approaching mid-channel. A slight deflection in one of its lower, compression

Below *The principle of the Forth Bridge demonstrated by Benjamin Baker sitting on the suspended span between his colleagues' cantilever arms.*

Below left *Although larger and more complex, the pneumatic caissons for the Forth Bridge foundations were developed from earlier wrought iron models like this.*

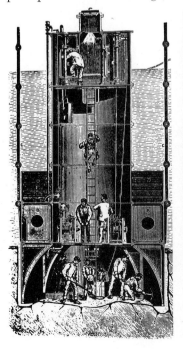

chords was noticed, but work continued. After repeated requests to Cooper and the Phoenix head-office for detailed advice, Cooper telegraphed the order for an inquiry and the resident engineer, Norman McClure stopped all construction work. McClure then left for New York to see Cooper in person. An unqualified superintendent on the bridge ordered work to proceed after McClure's departure. A few minutes before the end of the working day on August 29 1907, the faulty member gave way and the 19,000 tons of steel-work of the south arm collapsed, carrying 82 construction workers to their deaths.

In the long and agonizing Government inquiry, blame for the disaster was laid on the fundamental weakness in designing for economy rather than strength. Although there was a grave fault in the important compression members which actually gave way, the whole design was criticized for assuming a much too low dead load. But the disaster led to more general doubts; such as those voiced by the *Scientific American*:

The tremendous significance of this disaster lies in the suspicion which is staring every engineer coldly in the face, that there is something wrong with our theories of bridge design, at least as applied to a structure the size of the Quebec bridge.

A bridge at Quebec was still badly needed, so in 1908 a new board was formed by the Canadian Government and in 1910 a new design was chosen. The idea of an 1800 foot cantilever was retained, but the new bridge was to be far heavier and stronger and stiffened with 'K' bracing. It was also decided not to build the suspended span out from each cantilever arm, but to prefabricate it complete and hoist it 150 feet into position. In September 1916 the 20-hour lifting operation began and no sooner had the 5200 ton span lifted a few feet, than a casting supporting one of the

four hydraulic jacks failed, causing the Quebec Bridge's second tragedy. The failure put such uneven stresses into the truss that it folded up and plunged in to the St Lawrence River, carrying 11 workers with it. A year later an identical truss span was lifted into position with improved jacks. The four-day operation finally brought the world's longest cantilever span into being.

The immediate effect of the doubts cast by the Quebec disaster was to force bridge designers to look very closely indeed at the cantilever spans then under construction. One of these was the Queensboro or Blackwell's Island Bridge in New York which, in 1907, was nearly complete. Although the span was to be over 600 feet less than the Quebec Bridge, both the weight of the structure and its live loading were to be much greater. Where Quebec was to carry a road and a single track railway, Queensboro was being prepared to take on two decks; four streetcar tracks and four elevated railway tracks as well as the road and footpaths. The investigation that followed the Quebec failure concluded the bridge would not be able to hold itself and such an enormous live load up. Two of the rail tracks were removed and heavy concrete road paving was not laid.

The longer term effects of Quebec were twofold. First, much research was carried out on the design of large steel compression pieces. Second, canti-levers of great size were not attempted again for many years (although it could be argued that many years would pass before such long and heavy spans would actually be required again). In 1936 the East Bay Crossing at San Francisco was opened with two 1400 feet cantilever sections. In 1943, the New Howrah Bridge across the Hooghly in Calcutta reached a span of 1500 feet. The only significantly longer cantilever since then is the

Below An elegant French variation of the balanced cantilever—the Viaur Viaduct on the Toulouse and Lyons line—was built between 1896 and 1902. There is no suspended span between the cantilever arms.

Chester-Bridgeport Bridge over the Delaware River, with a span of 1644 feet, not opened until 1974.

Many others have been built, several with spans between 1000 and 1200 feet and, as from the beginning, the later development of the cantilever was closely bound up with progress in truss construction. Thus before considering some other cantilevers, we must return to the early days of the change-over from iron to steel.

Trusses

Major General William Sooy Smith was an American Army engineer, who in the 1870s, had carried out tests on comparative strengths of iron and steel. Steel had shown such favourable results, that Smith set out to build the world's first all steel bridge for the Chicago, Alton and St Louis railroad at Glasgow, over the Missouri River. Smith's bridge took just over a year to build and was opened in 1879. It consisted of five conventional Whipple-Murphy trusses, and was such an ordinary bridge in all other respects than its use of steel throughout, that it was largely ignored by the public. Engineers took a little more notice, and in ten years or so, steel had become the standard material for use in trusses.

The Glasgow Bridge and most other early steel trusses were required by the railways. Mostly these were plain, down-to-earth structures, relatively economic and straightforward to construct. Long bridges could be built simply by multiplying the number of separate truss units. Many of the best examples are still to be found in the United States, particularly in the work of a prolific designer, George S. Morison, who built seven Whipple-Murphy truss bridges over the Missouri River from 1880. The longest of these was the 1675 foot bridge at Sioux City with four 400 foot spans. However, plain trusses of many

Above *The wreckage of the south cantilever of the Quebec Bridge in August 1907. Eighty-two men died as a main compression member buckled and 19,000 tons of steelwork collapsed.*

Left *The Quebec Bridge was finally opened in 1918. Its single 1800 foot span took over the 'world's longest' title from the Forth Bridge. The suspended span of 630 feet, weighing over 5000 tons, took four days to lift into position.*

types were built the world over—like the Hawkesbury River Bridge, Australia, of 1889 and the Attock Bridge over the Indus in Pakistan, completed in 1883.

When something a little more special or decorative was required, a steel lenticular truss was sometimes used. The principle here is similar to Brunel's Saltash Bridge, with the top curved chord in compression held in by the lower curved chord in tension, with the deck suspended from

this lens-shaped combination. The most spectacular early example of this type was a three-span (330 feet each) bridge actually built of iron over the Elbe in Hamburg, which boasted an incredible pair of fairy castellated gateways at each end. Gustav Lindenthal chose the principle for a distinguished bridge to carry Smithfield street across the Monongahela River in Pittsburgh in 1887.

In building truss bridges of more than one span, however, it was realized that the spans could be made longer and stronger if the independent trusses could be joined together to form a continuous structure. Since each span can then act to anchor, or balance the load in its neighbour, a continuous truss girder bridge acts with a cantilever effect on adjacent spans. One interesting early example was the Boyne bridge, built in Ireland in 1885. Using the Town Lattice truss system, its two side spans of 140 feet each were, during erection, built continuous with the central 267 foot span. The bridge was completed by separating the spans; but later, when it was realized how much stronger a continuous structure was, they were riveted back together again.

The most monumental continuous truss ever built is Gustav Lindenthal's Sciotoville Bridge across the Ohio River near Portsmouth, Ohio. In 1914, the continuous truss was a novelty, but Lindenthal demonstrated with this bridge that fairly long spans could carry immense loads, given the continuous truss form and enough steel to build a very deep cross section. The two, symmetrical spans (navigation interests demanded two equal channels) are 775 feet each and, over the central pier, the truss is 128 feet deep. The Sciotoville was designed to carry 78,800 pounds per foot of combined live and dead load; the highest for any bridge.

The next type of bridge to consider is the next logical step from the 'pure' continuous truss—the combination of the truss and cantilever principles which was also developed in America. A truss acts like a simple beam with compression in its top chord and tension in its lower chord. In a cantilever, these stresses are reversed, so the way some of these bridges work is not always obvious. However, they were found to be economical and capable of longer spans than separate trusses. Although developed in Europe and elsewhere, the best examples come from the United States, often because the obstacles there were much larger and crossings and spans had to be longer.

One of the first bridges to combine the two principles was the Poughkeepsie Bridge over the Hudson. The deck to carry the Central Western and New England Railroad was supported on alternating trusses and cantilevers. The heavy trusses acted as counterbalances for the projecting cantilever arms.

Incidentally, the designer of the Poughkeepsie Bridge, Thomas Curtis Clarke, summed up the current US philosophy of bridge building—
Where so many bridges had to be built in a short time aesthetic considerations are little regarded. Utility alone governs their design. So long as they are strong enough, few care how they look. While his own Poughkeepsie Bridge was *not a thing of beauty . . . we hope it may be a joy forever to its stockholders.*

The more usual American combination was the 'through cantilever'. An early pioneer was George S. Morison in his 710 foot Mississippi River Bridge at Memphis in 1892, and the type reached its finest development in 1930 with Joseph B. Strauss's Longview Bridge over the Columbia River in Washington. In these cases the railway or road deck is supported on the bottom chords of main bearing cantilevers which are continuous with the linking trusses.

Left above *The Howrah Bridge in Calcutta, with a 1500 foot span, was completed in 1943. The 564 foot suspended span was built, like the Forth Bridge, continuous with the cantilever arms and joined at mid-span.*

Right above *The lenticular trusses of the Elbe Bridge in Hamburg were originally built in iron around 1882. Each grotesque set of girders spans 330 feet.*

Right centre *The Chesapeake and Ohio Railway bridge at Sciotoville, Ohio was designed by Gustav Lindenthal and completed in 1917. Only the specialist Indian 'High Steel Men' of New York were prepared to risk the construction work 200 feet above the Ohio River.*

Right below *The first Hawkesbury River Bridge in New South Wales was opened in 1889 and occupied the piers just beyond the present bridge. The foundations of the soft alluvial river bed were so poor that the replacement bridge was started in 1939.*

Above *Nanking road and rail bridge over the Yangtze River in the Peoples' Republic of China was opened in 1968. The continuous truss is divided into ten 425 foot spans. The upper deck carries two lanes for motor traffic, two footpaths and a pair of special bicycle lanes.*

Right *The truss and cantilever construction of the Richmond-San Raphael Bridge carries a two deck highway some four miles across the San Pablo Bay in California. In the middle of the bay, short, strong towers are necessary to counteract seismic movements, while the main channel spans have to be high enough for ship navigation. The deck, therefore, varies in level considerably over its central section.*

The use of this combination has lasted from the railway era through to the age of the automobile. Some of the gigantic highway bridges in the United States of the last two decades use the same principle. They underline the enormous pressures which motor transport puts on road systems to the point where it becomes economically feasible to invest huge sums of capital into projects to shorten road distances with larger and larger bridges. Like Thomas Clarke's bridge, most of these are not very beautiful, although one or two examples are worth singling out.

The Richmond-San Raphael Bridge, completed in 1956, carries the highway some four miles across the San Pablo Bay in California. The two navigation channels required by the Navy had to have 185 feet and 135 feet headroom respectively. However, money was saved in the design by providing the clearance only under the two main cantilevered spans. For the remainder of the bridge the road is carried in trusses at a much lower level and consequently the bridge has a remarkable roller-coaster profile.

The three miles of the Tappan Zee Bridge carries the New York State Thruway across the widest point of the Hudson River, between Tarrytown and Nyak. The Port of New York Authority would not permit a bridge any further downstream towards New York City which would have been perhaps more convenient for drivers and certainly easier for the constructors. In this case the main problem was the prohibitive depth of solid rock for founding for the deep water piers, including those for the main cantilever truss spans. The unique solution was to sink into the soft river bed alluvium ten huge hollow concrete caissons which would be buoyant enough (assisted by a few steel piles driven down to bedrock) to support 80 percent of the bridge's dead weight.

The cantilever/truss combination is not exclusive to the United States. In Nanking, China, in 1968 a double-deck bridge was opened over the Yangtze River, providing a direct road and rail link between Shanghai and Peking. Ten river spans carry a continuous truss over three-quarters of a mile, with a two lane highway on the upper deck and a double track railway line on the lower. While a similar bridge was constructed in 1956 at Wuhan with Russian assistance, the Yangtze River Bridge was built entirely by the Chinese, using steel from the Anshan works in Manchuria fabricated at the Shanhaikwan Bridge Works.

Moving bridges

One of the most serious problems which face engineers planning bridges over wide and deep bodies of water is that such water is usually navigable by large ships. Not only has the engineer got to construct a long span, but he has to leave shipping with enough headroom to use the waterway. The problem is frequently made worse by the fact that many navigable waterways are rivers and estuaries situated in fairly flat country.

Thus, to build a bridge with sufficient headroom often involves constructing long and expensive high approaches. This is especially necessary for railways, which can only operate with very gentle gradients.

The solution to this type of problem is often a moving bridge—the approaches can be kept to a minimum height, the amount of material in the bridge can also be minimized, and the span simply shifted out of the way for ships to pass. The problem, of course, then, is to build a span long enough to bridge the channel, and consequently to have machinery strong and reliable enough to move the structure when necessary. Add to these, the necessity of having the bridge and its complex heavy machinery constantly being maintained and continually manned for operation, and we have the main reasons for the moving bridge being fairly rare. A moveable bridge is thus a relatively expensive alternative and one which will only be really useful if traffic is light enough to be interrupted when necessary.

The four main types of moveable bridge—the bascule, swing, vertical lift and transporter—all depended upon steel for their development. Firstly, the ratio of strength to weight of steel made practicable spans which were long and strong enough to be useful and at the same time light enough to be moved. Secondly, the technology associated with steel production enabled the development of engines and motors capable of shifting the spans, as well as the development of bearings tough enough to withstand movement of such large structures. Developments in the four types of moveable bridge have not been in any particular chronological order, although it is true that fewer and fewer moveable bridges are being built today, and many, especially those carrying railways, are becoming used less and less.

The most ancient in principle is the bascule or drawbridge, originally used as a defensive measure. The drawbridge of a medieval castle was simply hinged at its base and hauled up when necessary. The amount of effort required to raise a drawbridge can be drastically cut if the bridge is counterbalanced, with the hinge nearer the span's centre of gravity. Many ingenious forms of counterbalancing were developed by Dutch bridge builders for their canal spans, so that quite heavy structures could be shifted by one person.

Although there are modern bascule bridges in many parts of the world, the most famous bridge of this type is Tower Bridge in London. Both Captain Samuel Brown and Thomas Telford had proposed high level bridges early in the nineteenth century, and had their plans turned down because of the difficulty and expense of constructing the approaches. London continued to grow eastwards and the pressure of traffic on London Bridge became more and more acute, so that in 1885 a Bill was passed to construct the new bridge downstream, near the Tower. The Tower Bridge was financed by the Corporation of the City from the funds of the Bridge Estates, built up over the centuries for Old London Bridge.

The architect for the bridge planned the bizarre towers to blend with the Tower of London, and although to the modern eye the turrets, gables and decorated windows do nothing of the kind, Horace Jones was knighted by the Prince of Wales for his design. The function of the towers is in fact to support the steelwork suspending the side spans. The hydraulic machinery for raising and lowering each of the 1100 ton bascules is housed in the large piers at the base of each tower, and is capable of fully opening the bridge in under four minutes. The reliability of the lifting gear powered primarily by the London Hydraulic main is famous. The only near disaster to have occurred was the stranding of a number 78 bus across the widening gap as the bridge was being raised on one occasion in 1952. The auxiliary steam driven machinery on the bridge has now all been replaced save one engine which is kept for historical purposes.

The pivots for the lifting spans of Tower Bridge are roller trunnion bearings, similar in principle to those used for raising and lowering the barrels of early types of cannon. However, many bascule bridges use the patent Scherzer roller bearing as a pivot. In this type the lifting spans rock backwards as they rise on a geared track. Early advertising for this kind of bearing made much of its advantage of being able to leave the whole

width of the channel clear. Most American bascules were built in this way, including the central moving section of the Arlington Memorial Bridge in Washington, D.C. The fewer examples in the United Kingdom include railway bridges at Carmarthen and at Keady, over the River Trent.

The width of channel that can be left clear by a moving bridge is crucial, and one of the main disadvantages of a swing bridge is that in midspan it requires a large pier on which to rotate. This, however, did not deter engineers on the Bridgewater canal. In the 1890s, James Brindley's famous stone aqueduct over the River Irwell had to be replaced when the river was developed into part of the Manchester Ship Canal. A swing bridge was devised to carry a 230 foot section of the canal in a steel trough, pivoted on bearings on a small island in the ship canal. The trough full of water weighs 1500 tons and requires a pair of special hydraulically operated gates to seal the water in when in operation.

A larger and more recent example is the swing bridge over the Caronte Canal at Port de Boue in France. The original swing bridge was destroyed by the Germans in 1944. The railway line it carried was re-opened in 1948 with a pair of temporary vertical lift structures. With these in continual operation, the permanent replacement could be constructed *in situ*. The swing truss was

Below Tower Bridge shown in action soon after its completion in 1894. In its heyday ships (taking precedence over road users by Act of Parliament) could summon the raising of the counterpoised bascules with one long and three short blasts of the siren. Nowadays, the Bridge Master requires 24 hours notice for a lift.

cantilevered out from its concrete tower, parallel to the canal, and at right angles to the line, with trains running through a gap left in the centre of the truss work. When complete, the vertical lifts were removed and the 365 foot new bridge swung into use on its ring of 63 steel roller bearings.

In vertical lift bridges, the span carrying the road or railway is kept level as it is lifted to the top of towers at either end of the span. Huge counterweights on pulleys balance the load of the span so that the net energy required in lifting and lowering can be minimized. The towers, machinery, weights and pulleys necessary for this type of bridge often make them extremely ugly. Many examples in the eastern United States, like the Newark Bay bridge and the trio over the Hakensack River, Jersey City, fall into this category. Incidentally, on September 15 1958 a train ran through all the signals while the Newark Bay spans were lifted. It plunged into the bay and 48 people died, including the locomotive crew—why they did not stop has never been established.

Two vertical lift bridges of less hideous aspect are the Cape Cod Canal Bridge at Buzzards Bay which carries a section of the Penn Central Railroad to Cape Cod. A firm of architects, McKim, Mead and White, were given the specific responsibility of making the towers as pleasing as they

could. Given the maritime location, they chose a lighthouse motif, and took great care to keep the cables, pulleys and winding gear well out of sight. Considering the size of the span—540 feet—the result was very successful, but, like many railway bridges, it is used much less nowadays than at its completion in 1935.

Even neater, is the Kingsferry-Sheppey lift bridge in Kent, England which was opened in 1960 to replace an earlier bascule bridge. Here, apparently solid reinforced concrete towers completely hide the control room, cables and counterbalance weights. The electric motors in each tower can raise the 90 foot span to 130 feet clearance in 90 seconds.

The other type of moving bridge is the transporter bridge or 'ferry bridge' as it is sometimes known. In this case the bridge, either a cantilever or suspension span, supports a high-level horizontal railway for a moving trolley from which is suspended a short section of road deck, which is ferried from shore to shore. There was something of a vogue for these bridges in the first decade of this century, but the conditions requiring them are so infrequent that they are very rare. One of the classics of this type was the 787 foot span 'pont transbordeur' across Marseilles harbour, constructed in 1905 by the engineer Arnodin. The

Above The site of Brindley's Barton Aqueduct carrying the Bridgewater Canal over the River Irwell. It was replaced in 1893 by a swing aqueduct to allow the passage of the large craft on the new Manchester Ship Canal.

Left above *The vertical lift is often the only method of moving spans long enough to cross the large inland waterways for sea-going shipping.*

Left below *The Houghton Hancock Bridge (1959) in North Michigan has a double deck lifting span and a clearance of 100 feet when required.*

same year saw the erection of the Widnes and Runcorn 1000 foot transporter in England, and the ferry bridge across the harbour mouth at Duluth in America. The rails for the travelling cradle are supported in these structures, either by cantilevers or by suspended trusses. Although they have great curiosity value, they are severely limited in the load they can carry, and are becoming rarer. The Runcorn/Widnes bridge, for example, has already been replaced by a trussed arch.

Finally, in the steel section must be included the Bailey Bridge. This system of bridge construction was developed during the Second World War when armoured vehicles became too heavy for the British Army's available temporary bridges. In 1941 Sir Donald Bailey introduced his new system which has proved to be extremely versatile and as useful in peacetime as in battle. The basic unit of the system is a prefabricated truss panel 10 feet long, designed for handling by six men. These panels can be fitted together in a large number of different combinations, depending on the obstacle to be crossed, and on the eventual load to be carried.

For the heaviest loads, up to three panels can be joined on top of one another to create a deep truss. For longer spans, panels can be fixed together to form a continuous truss which can then be suspended from steel cables. Where dry foundations can be found, the Bailey crib pier can be used for intermediate support. For crossing water Bailey designed pontoons which, combined with special hinged truss sections, could be erected in a very short time.

The carrying capacity of 100 tons over 220 foot spans and the flexibility of the system were first demonstrated by the British Army in the North African campaign in 1942, and subsequently used by both British, and later, American forces in Europe. Since the Second World War, the system has been much used where temporary bridges have been required in cases of accident and floods or during the construction of permanent works.

Above *Pre-fabricated units can be easily erected to form a bridge in an emergency. The best-known of these types is the Bailey Bridge developed by the British Army in the Second World War.*

Suspension Bridges

SINCE 1929 ALL the world's longest spans have been suspension bridges. The story of their development, however, stretches from the pioneering work of Finlay, Telford and Brown with iron and stone, right up to the high technology of the giant spans of today in steel and concrete; from an age of the heroic engineer to today's co-ordinated efforts of teams of specialists. Suspension bridges are capable of huge spans for road traffic, and their evolution has broadly kept pace with the rise of motor transport, although many of the basic ideas were established during the later railway era.

The suspension bridge story is largely an American one, although much of the early experimental work was carried out in France, and the very latest ideas are the result of British research and development. After Brown's technique of using a chain of eyebars to carry the suspended road, the next really important step was the alternative technique of employing a number of iron wires to take the load.

A similar method (using $\frac{1}{2}$-inch iron bars) had been suggested by Telford as early as 1814 in his original plans for the Widnes/Runcorn span that was never built. In 1816, however, the first wire cable suspension bridges appeared—one in the United States, at Fairmont, Philadelphia, by White and Hasard and one in Britain at Gala-shiels, where a 112 foot span was built by Redpath and Brown. Cables for these bridges had been hauled into position complete, but in 1829, M. Vicat put up a small bridge over the Rhône

in France using the unprecedented method of spinning these wire cables *in situ* on the bridge.

One of the greatest problems of suspended spans from their earliest days has been the dangers associated with their flexibility. A few weeks after the opening of the Menai Bridge, observers and engineers had been alarmed at the movement of the bridge deck during a gale. Suspended spans required the development of the stiffening truss to reach longer spans, and again, some of the important early-work was done in France, particularly by Marc Seguin. In 1840 he had built a 137 foot suspended span over the Saône. Although his railway bridge was a short-lived temporary structure, built for use pending completion of a permanent stone bridge, its trusses foreshadowed later developments.

The United States

America's subsequent lead in the design and construction of suspension bridges was largely due to the work of two men; Colonel Charles Ellet (1810–1862) and John Augustus Roebling (1806–1869). Ellet, an unconventional and innovatory character, was born in Bristol, Pennsylvania and demonstrated a precocious talent in, among other subjects, mathematics and languages. At 18, he had bluffed his way into an assistant engineer's job on the Chesapeake and Ohio Canal—his employers thought he was 22 and fully trained. In 1830, he went to France and studied at the Ecole Polytechnique. There he met several of the

eminent French bridge builders and realized the potential of the iron-wire suspension bridge. When he returned to America, aged 22, he submitted a proposal for a 1000 foot bridge over the Potomac River in Washington (the Menai was currently the world's longest clear span at 570 feet), but this was never built. His first important bridge, however, was a replacement for the old Colossus Bridge at Fairmount, which had burned down in 1838. Ellet's bridge, built between 1841 and 1842, was the first successful wire-cable suspension span built in the United States, though its span was a modest 358 feet.

Ellet got his chance to build the first thousand foot bridge in 1846. This was the Wheeling Bridge over the Ohio River, with its record 1010 foot span to be suspended 97 feet above river level. As the bridge neared completion in 1849 a long series of legal battles began, largely brought about by steamboat and rival railway interests. A Supreme Court ruling that the clearance of the bridge should be increased to an impossible 111 feet was eventually reversed in 1852 by President Fillmore. However, the citizens of Wheeling and neighbouring Belmont had enjoyed their bridge only two years, when, on a windy day in May 1854, it collapsed. Ellet's contemporary and rival designer John A. Roebling commented that the collapse was *clearly owing to a want of stability and not a want of strength. This want of stiffness could have been supplied by over-floor stays, truss railings, underfloor stays or cable stays.* It seems that these comments were taken to heart in rebuilding the

Wheeling Bridge in the form it now takes, although it is not certain exactly who had formal responsibility for the reconstruction.

Roebling had submitted plans for the original Wheeling Bridge, but had been turned down. In the same year 1846, Roebling and Ellet were again rivals in the contract to design a railway bridge over the Niagara. At the time, a suspension span was the only possible solution to crossing the 1000 foot gorge. Iron trusses were in their infancy, great cantilevers and arches undreamed of, and timber and stone were ruled out because of the impossibility of founding piers or of erecting false-work over the raging eddies of the waters below the Niagara Falls. Ellet again won the contract.

This time, with the two great contracts under his belt, Ellet was thus the most renowned suspension bridge designer in North America. However, he managed to construct a foot bridge over Niagara before a disagreement over its toll revenues forced his resignation from the project. In 1853, Roebling's alternative suspension designs were accepted and he took the project over.

One of the other designs which had been considered by the railway company had been based on Robert Stephenson's tubular box girder principle used in the Victoria project over the St Lawrence river. Roebling's Niagara bridge was opened on January 1 1855 and finally established his pre-eminence over Ellet. It was a two-deck structure with a main span of 821 feet 4 inches suspended from four $10\frac{1}{4}$ inch diameter wire

Below *Roebling's Niagara Suspension Bridge of 1855 carried road and rail 821 feet across the Falls. This bridge was the exception to the rule that suspension spans were not suitable for railways. When it was opened in 1855, the truss work was timber. The much modified bridge lasted until 1897 when loads were becoming too heavy for it.*

cables. The upper deck carried the railway, and the lower deck carried a roadway. In his final report to the bridge company in May 1855, Roebling put down the success of his structure to . . . *weight, girders, trusses and stays. With these, any degree of stiffness can be insured, to resist either the action of trains; or the violence of storms or even hurricanes* . . . With time, Roebling's structure had to be renovated, due mainly to wear and tear caused by the continuous vibrating loads of railway trains. First, damaged wires in the cables had to be replaced, then, in 1880, the original timber trusses were swapped for steel ones. Finally, in 1897, the whole bridge had to be replaced due to increasing loading from heavier and heavier trains. However, on its completion some 40 years earlier, it had proved the economic and technical feasibility of suspension bridges for long spans carrying heavy loads. It established Roebling as the one man who properly understood the roles of weight and trusses as essential ingredients of the successful, rigid suspension bridge.

John A. Roebling had been born in Mulhausen in Germany and he was educated at the Royal Politechnic School, Berlin, in engineering and architecture. After several attempts, he and a small group of friends succeeded in escaping from the anti-liberal backlash in Germany resulting from the French revolts of 1830.

He landed in America in 1831, aged 25, and began life in the new land as a farmer. His ambition and qualifications, however, led him away from the land to seek opportunities with the developing American canal companies. The story is told that while working on the canals, Roebling witnessed a dreadful accident when a rope for hauling barges on special trucks up inclined planes snapped and crushed two men to death in the wreck. Roebling began work on a method of manufacturing wire hawsers, flexible enough to be wound on a winch but many times as strong as vegetable fibre. His wire ropes proved so useful for many purposes, including much safer canal portages that they won Roebling an immediate local reputation, and eventually led him to open

The Cincinnati-Covington Bridge, with a span of 1057 feet over the Ohio River, was opened in 1866 after 20 years of difficulties including the Civil War. This picture shows the bridge as Roebling designed it, before the drastic re-building with steel cables and trusses in 1899.

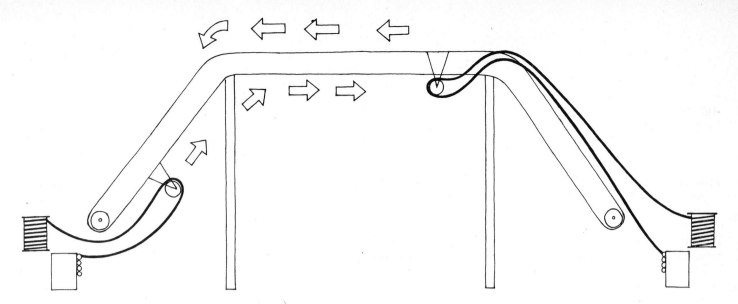

in 1849 what was to become a huge manufacturing plant at Trenton, New Jersey.

Since his student days in Berlin, Roebling had been fascinated by the notion of suspension bridges. He had written a graduation thesis analyzing a small Bavarian structure he had come across. During the 1840s he combined this interest with his knowledge of working with iron wire, to design several suspended aqueducts for various canal companies. One, which is still standing, was the Delaware aqueduct of 1848 across the Delaware River at Lackawaxen, Pennsylvania. Continuous iron cables were strung, one wire at a time, across four spans about 135 feet each. Although it was later converted into a highway bridge, in its original form it did demonstrate the load-carrying capacity of suspension spans.

Roebling was convinced that wire cable suspension bridges were the most practicable and economic solutions for the spans that the burgeoning New World communities so desperately needed. From the mid-forties, he built several bridges to prove his point—most notably, a bridge over the Monongahela River, Pittsburgh (later replaced by Lindenthal's Smithfield Street lenticular trusses), the Niagara Bridge mentioned earlier and the Cincinnati-Covington Bridge.

The building of the Cincinnati Bridge was a twenty-year saga, the first ten years of which were spent in argument and lobbying for and against Roebling's original proposals, first put to the Bridge Company in 1846. The capital could not be raised—most of the gold from the 1849 Californian gold rush was poured into the railways—not into road bridge projects. The steamboat companies mounted a huge campaign scaremongering about the fragility of Roebling's plan for a 1057 foot suspension bridge. The only alternative, a multi-span bridge would also be unacceptable:

If piers were placed in the river, water would be dammed up, the banks would be flooded, and the city would be ruined. Navigation on the Ohio would be obstructed and real property values in Cincinnati would be destroyed.

When the project did get off the ground in 1856, every kind of problem was encountered. Excavations were flooded, work was stopped when the river froze, a national financial crash dried up all the funds, and last but not least, the Civil War broke out in 1860 and work all but ceased. Against all these odds, the masonry towers were finished in September 1865, the four cables strung in several months, and the bridge ready for vehicular traffic by January 1867.

These last stages of the work were supervised on the site by Roebling's son, Colonel Washington A. Roebling. He had been trained by his father and had studied at the Rensselaer Politechnic Institute before enlisting in the Union Army in the Civil War, during which he had designed and built two suspension bridges of his own. Father and son were to go on to build one of the greatest landmarks in the history of bridges—the Brooklyn Bridge over the East River in New York.

The idea for a bridge across the East River had been discussed since the early days of the century, but it was not until John Roebling submitted a detailed proposal in 1867 that the project looked at all possible. Even then, many people simply would not believe that a 1600 foot suspension bridge could be built, and ten years passed before a company was formed to turn Roebling's plan into reality. That ten years, while the Covington-Cincinnati bridge was going up was spent by Roebling working out every detail, so that only two months after he was officially appointed engineer to the project, work could have begun. However, two more years of reporting and lobbying, discussion and examination passed before the go-ahead was actually given.

Roebling himself had no doubts; he wrote: *The completed structure will be not only the greatest work of the continent, and of the age . . . . As a great work of art, and as a successful specimen of advanced bridge engineering, this structure will forever testify to the energy, enterprise and wealth of that community which shall secure its erection.* His basic plan was for huge monumental masonry towers, bearing for the first time, steel cables from which would be suspended a strong iron truss.

Above The cable spinning technique first perfected by the Roeblings has since been used on all steel cable suspension spans. For each cable, a pair of travelling sheaves on an endless loop of rope is hauled back and forth. On each crossing, each sheave carries a strand of cable wire, with one end anchored and the other unwinding from a supply bobbin. Four strands are thus laid at each traverse and are anchored securely before a fresh strand is looped around the sheaves for the return trip.

This stiffening would, Roebling maintained, be strong enough to hold itself up, without the cables. *The bridge would sink in the centre, but would not fall.*

In June 1869, just three days after final authorization for the bridge, tradegy struck. John Roebling, while surveying the exact position for the Brooklyn Tower, missed his footing and had his right foot crushed by a docking ferry. Three weeks later, he died from tetanus before ground had been broken for his greatest project. If the bridge was to be built, the New York Bridge Company had no choice but to appoint the 32-year-old Washington Roebling, who knew every detail of the design, in his father's place. Over the next 14 years, the younger Roebling sacrificed his health and strength to the great work.

Like Captain Eads, then in the middle of constructing the St Louis Bridge, Washington had been to Europe to study the pneumatic caisson method for digging underwater foundations. He also had the benefit of Eads' own experience. To support the 280 foot towers, the Brooklyn caissons had to be enormous. They took the form of huge, partitioned timber boxes, 108 by 168 feet in which gangs of workmen could work under compressed air, excavating the river bed, so the caisson would gradually sink to solid rock under its own weight plus that of masonry laid inside. When founded on rock any remaining spaces would be filled with concrete and more masonry. With this technique of working at great depths still in its infancy, every kind of difficulty was encountered at the bottom of the East River. In those days before electric light, gas burners had to be used for lighting the working chambers. In the compressed air there was thus a terrific fire risk. The Brooklyn caissons sustained several fires, culminating in the 'great fire' of December 1870, which set the work back three months. Among other difficulties, were the compacted river bed, with a number of large boulders, and the tendency of the caissons to 'blow out'. This happened when the air pressure in them reached a point when it forced showers of mud, sand and stones up and out of the water locks used for removing excavated material from the caisson.

By far the most serious problem, however, on the New York tower foundation was the still little-understood 'caisson disease'. By May 1872, three men had died with the caisson at 78 feet down, and with some way still to go. Roebling decided that the caisson should go on deeper, but before the concrete filling was complete, Roebling

Below *The Roeblings' crossing of New York's East River with the Brooklyn Bridge is one of the greatest stories in bridge building and the greatest triumph of nineteenth century American engineering. The building of its 1600 foot span, suspended from steel wire cables, was a continuous battle from 1869 to 1883 against personal tragedy, natural disasters, unforeseen technical problems and graft.*

himself, who spent most of his time in the caissons with the workmen, suffered a paralyzing attack of 'the bends' which nearly killed him. For the next 11 years Roebling, unable to write, and in considerable pain, had to direct operations on the bridge from a distance—first from the family house in Trenton, later from a house in Brooklyn in sight of the bridge.

Many questions were raised about Roebling's ability to continue as chief engineer, but the original plans had in fact been made so well that Roebling was well able to cope with technical matters. His uncanny understanding of events that took place on the site amazed the engineers and constructors actually doing the work.

He faced two great problems in building the superstructure. Firstly, there was a battle with the Company over the contracts for supplying the steel wire for the cables. The suppliers chosen by the Company did not, in fact, provide wire to Roebling's exacting specifications, and had to make good their fraud at their own expense on Roebling's insistence. Secondly, with the bridge nearly complete in 1881, Roebling had to add 1000 tons of extra steelwork to the trusses to make the bridge strong enough to carry a railway. Although steam trains never actually ran over the

bridge, this late decision to strengthen it allowed it to carry ever-increasing traffic loads for 75 years, without any structural alterations.

The Brooklyn Bridge, the world's longest span, at nearly 1600 feet, the first suspension bridge with steel cables, was also the first bridge over the East River and was thus a milestone in the history of the city of New York. The civic celebrations on its opening on May 24 1883 were unparalleled, but Washington Roebling stayed at home and received a delegation of friends, fellow engineers and officials after the ceremonies.

These were still the early days of building in steel, and despite the success of the Brooklyn Bridge, the suspension principle was not proven as the best solution to long spans, especially for railway loads. The Forth Rail Bridge and later the Quebec cantilevers took over the 'world's longest' titles from 1889 to 1929. However, from the turn of the century, the technology of wire-cable suspension bridges was gradually developed and refined in progressively longer and longer spans. The second East River bridge, the Williamsburg, completed in 1903, was the first major suspension bridge to use steel towers. Its 1600 foot span was designed by Lefferts L. Buck who specialized in arches, and it represented the

Below right The walkway over Brooklyn Bridge. The original steelwork of the cables and trusses survived hugely increasing traffic loads for more than 60 years. The strengthening of the bridge and the widening of the traffic lanes in 1948 were designed very carefully to avoid altering the bridge's original appearance.

ultimate in truss stiffening with its 40 foot panels. Simultaneously the Manhattan Bridge project was begun and a design by O. F. Nichols was constructed, featuring a shallower stiffening truss and more flexible steel towers. Early on in the project there had been an argument over whether to build using the European eyebar principle. Gustav Lindenthal, then in charge of the project had cited the 951 foot span of the Elizabeth Bridge in Budapest (1903) as a precedent. His proposal had been dropped on the grounds of the obstruction to East River traffic which would have been caused by the necessary falsework for an eyebar bridge.

In 1926 came what must be called the first modern suspension bridge, the Philadelphia-Camden Bridge, better known as the Benjamin Franklin Bridge over the Delaware River. Designed by Ralph Modjeski, it incorporated all the known refinements of suspension bridge building of the time, and featured a 1750 foot span, with handsome diagonal braced steel towers, and relatively low Warren truss stiffening. In 1929 came the Ambassador Bridge in Detroit, the longest span in the world, finally topping the Quebec by 50 feet. Problems on this and the contemporary Mount Hope Bridge, Rhode Island, were encountered with the heat-treated wire being used in the cables. Although laboratory trials had suggested this wire was superior to cold drawn wire, under the repeated vibration caused by the travelling sheaves spinning the cable, strands had started to split and fail. Cold drawn wire has been used ever since.

Greater spans, however, were imminent, and three bridges, completed within the next decade would set a new standard in long spans. These were the George Washington in New York (1931) the West Bay (1936) and the Golden Gate (1937), both in San Francisco.

The George Washington Bridge was designed in the main by Othmar H. Ammann, who had been born in Schaffhausen in Switzerland, and had arrived in the United States in 1904. He worked with Lindenthal between 1912 and 1923, and had been appointed to the Port of New York Authority in 1924, as chief engineer.

As the East River had cut off New York from Brooklyn, so the Hudson River was a tremendous barrier between New York and its western suburbs and satellites. The problem was that any bridge across the Hudson would have to be double the length of any existing span. Engineers since Roebling had maintained that the 3000 foot span was possible, but it was not until 1925 that the chance came to test the theory.

Practically every eminent bridge builder was consulted on the project, and Ammann's eventual plan contained three main features of interest. First, given the enormous length of the span, the sheer weight of the deck and of the necessarily huge cables could be enough to ensure rigidity. Second, the bridge could be constructed in two stages, first with a single deck, then later, as traffic increased, a second, lower deck could be

118

Left above *The Manhattan Bridge completed in 1909, was the fourth bridge over New York's East River. After work had begun on the foundations, designs were completely revised twice. The 1470 feet span actually built was an advanced concept.*

Left below *During the 1920s several American bridges, in quick succession, held the record for the world's longest suspended span. In 1926 it was the turn of the 1750 foot span of the Philadelphia-Camden Bridge over the Delaware River—now known as the Benjamin Franklin Bridge.*

Right above *The George Washington Bridge over the Hudson River in New York opened in 1931, with a single deck spanning 3500 feet. An important part of the bridge's planning was the design of the approach roads and toll gates.*

added on with a truss. Third, the side spans were to be short, with their cables stretched relatively tightly to their anchorages, providing even more stiffness.

The George Washington bridge, with its 3500 foot span doubling the previous record, was built in just four years. Work began in 1927 on an almost ideal site—one pier is on dry land and thus no deep excavations were necessary, since bedrock was not far below the surface. The 635 foot towers were built one 50 foot storey at a time. One hundred and seven thousand miles of wire were spun into the two cables in just 209 working days. The original design had called for monumental concrete cladding to be laid on the steel framework of the towers. In 1928, it was decided to save time and money by leaving the concrete off. Controversy over the aesthetic effect of the naked steel towers has raged ever since, but the bridge was opened in 1931—one whole year ahead of schedule.

Two other planning aspects of the bridge were important. The bridge over the Hudson was such an enormous and costly undertaking that, for the first time, private finance was not used. The Port Authority itself issued the bonds that would gradually be paid off from the proceeds of the bridge's tolls. Also, the bridge was the first major example of a co-ordinated bridge-and-highway development specifically for the motor car. Thirty-seven percent of the cost of the bridge in fact went into building approach roads, with one

way systems, easy gradients, and a number of planned links with major and local roads.

San Francisco Bay

On the other side of the United States, even larger projects were afoot. The area round San Francisco contained some of the fastest growing communities in the country. The great natural harbours of the San Francisco, Oakland and San Pablo Bays offered, at the same time, the area's most useful and attractive features and the most serious obstacles to local communications. The first great bridging schemes had been proposed by an amiable eccentric called Joshua Norton who in 1857 had declared himself Emperor of the United States and Mexico. One of his suggestions was for a link between San Francisco and Oakland, which until 1936 was an eight mile ferry boat journey.

By 1928 there had been no fewer than 38 proposals from private companies interested in constructing bridge systems across the Bay. For a long time the War Department refused to contemplate allowing a franchise for bridges across the bay, but eventually relented as problems of isolation, and congestion became acute in the two communities. In 1929, following New York's lead, the State of California took on the responsibility for creating the bridges, when President Hoover set up a special commission for the project.

There followed several years of studies and proposals. The main obstacle was the 10,000 foot crossing over West Bay between Yerba Buena Island and San Francisco itself. The commission stipulated no more than four spans, and those to harmonize with the scenic beauty of the bay. The War Department, of course, stipulated 135 foot headroom as usual. A fantastic array of alternative ideas was submitted, based on various combinations of suspended spans. One idea was for two main spans, with their cables suspended from one huge, central tower. Another was for a single bridge of 4100 feet with very long side spans. The scheme that was eventually adopted in 1932 was for two complete suspension bridges, back to back, sharing a common anchorage in mid-stream. It would have two 2310 foot main spans and a total of 8100 feet of double deck under cable. As originally conceived, it would have carried six lanes of traffic on the top deck and three lanes and two railway tracks on the lower deck.

As America was clawing its way out of the Depression, the money came from the Reconstruction Finance Commission, ($79,500,000 all told), and the bridge was built between 1933 and 1936. The East Bay leg of the bridge consisted of two through cantilevers of 1400 feet each. These were major spans in themselves, but they were overshadowed by the West Bay suspended spans and the bridge's staggering 43,500 foot total length.

Simultaneously, San Francisco's other great bridging project was under way. The need for a crossing over the Golden Gate between San Francisco and Sausalito was not so pressing as for the Transbay Bridge, but proposals again went back to the early years of the century. In 1916 a local journalist, James H. Wilking, had stirred up interest in a bridge project and, after a lapse for the First World War, the engineer Joseph B. Strauss had been asked to submit plans to the San Francisco Chief Engineer, in 1919. Strauss was born and educated in Cincinnati and some versions of his biography emphasize his short stature and the unpleasant experiences at college football which had led him to vow to achieve great things. Until the Golden Gate project, he had specialized in moving bridges and had built many bascules and vertical lift spans. From his office in Chicago he had designed bridges in Japan, Egypt, South America, Denmark and Imperial Russia.

His first proposal for the Golden Gate however was a monstrous cantilever suspension hybrid which embarrassed the San Francisco engineering office and outraged the public. Many years of arguments, lawsuits and submissions to the War Department followed. By the time the Golden Gate Company was formed, Strauss had come round to the idea of a suspended bridge, and another great team of consulting engineers was assembled which was unanimous for the concept. One of them was O. H. Ammann, whom Strauss had assisted in the George Washington project.

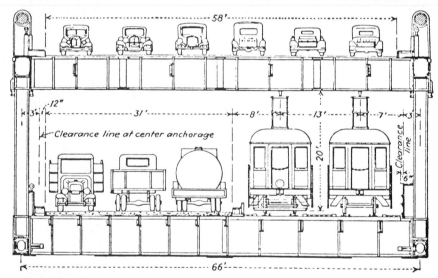

The plan eventually agreed called for a 4200 foot main span, so that one of the piers could be founded on a rock ledge, leaving only one to be founded in the deep treacherous waters of the harbour entrance. A team of 100 specialists—geologists, metallurgists and detailers—prepared and submitted final plans, but the project ran into serious opposition when the bonds to finance the work were issued. In the troubled economic climate following the Wall Street crash, many businessmen and investors considered a $35,000,000 bridge project a waste of money. However, there was just enough support to enable work to begin in January 1933.

By that time, Strauss had worn himself out in all the efforts to begin work on the bridge and, once construction began, he kept himself in the background. He had in fact suffered a breakdown in 1933, and his subsequent inconspicuousness led to rumours that he was not the principle figure behind the work that had been some 14 years in preparation. His colleagues on the job, however, had no such doubts.

In putting up the bridge, the main difficulty was the founding of the deep water pier. The site lay some 1125 feet from the shore in what was virtually open sea, unprotected from the $7\frac{1}{2}$ knot tidal currents, choppy seas and the large ships

entering and leaving the harbour. The unique solution to this problem was to sink a large, concrete cylinder on the sea bed, to act as a seawall and fender to protect a caisson working inside. However, before the caisson could be sunk properly, a storm blew up and bounced it around inside the cylinder with such force that the fender ring was threatened with destruction. The caisson was removed and the pier foundation made, simply by filling the cylindrical fender with concrete. This concrete pier was then resting on a layer of slippery, hard Serpentine clay. A famous geological controversy ensued over the question whether, in an earthquake, the pier would slide off the Serpentine or, in fact, be held steady as the base rock would be able to move independently below the clay. So far, the south pier of the Golden Gate has held firm.

Next came the construction of the tallest suspension bridge towers ever built. At 746 feet,

the steel, stepped back towers of Golden Gate gave the cables a very pronounced 'sag'. For the spinning of the cables, many special safety precautions were taken, including a specially trained and equipped team of doctors and nurses. They were on constant standby for any emergency from dealing with broken limbs to handing out special sunglasses for the workers on the towers and cables, many of whom suffered from dazzle and giddiness. Most importantly, a safety net was stretched the length of the bridge, and saved 19 falling workers over the period of cabling. Disaster occurred however as the bridge neared completion, when some scaffolding on the deck collapsed, carrying ten men and most of the safety net into the sea. Even so, the safety record was good; at the time construction workers had a rule of thumb which reckoned on one life lost per $1 million worth of structure.

The Golden Gate Bridge was opened in May 1937 with a full week of civic celebrations. Its size, of course, is proverbial and for 27 years it was the world's longest span—its natural setting is magnificent and its permanent coat of vermilion paint is a great attraction for San Franciscans and visitors alike. Aesthetic judgements have been pronounced against the excessive sag of the cables, the plainness of the stiffening trusses and the affected architectural style of the towers. For ordinary people, however, the bridge was a triumph, a symbol, once again, of man's mastery over nature and that particularly American belief that technology could cope with anything. This was the heyday of the suspension bridge but trouble was in store.

Failures in design

Ever since the days of Roebling and Ellet, bridge designers had been aware of the necessity, with suspension bridges, of keeping the roadway deck stiff. In the Williamsburg this was done with very deep trusses. Since that bridge, the trend in design had been towards more pleasing and economical shapes with shallower stiffening members and slender towers. In the long spans, like the George Washington, the sheer dead load of the bridge was enough to keep it rigid. In 1935, engineers attempted to establish ways of computing 'coefficients of stiffness' and to define what was acceptable for safety. Despite such computations it was still thought possible to construct safe suspension spans with a very low coefficient of stiffness, but the limit in fact was simply not known.

The main items in the design equation were the width of the road, the depth of the stiffening, and the force of the wind. When considering the first two parameters, the wind was thought of simply as an extra loading, not as a continually moving, eddying force that might have cumulative effects. The width of the road, or the distance between cables was important to prevent the deck being blown too far sideways. The rule of thumb for road width was that it should be around 1/30

of the span. As well as expecting some lateral movement, suspension bridge designers also expected some rather more dangerous vertical movements—to counter these, the rule of thumb was that the depth of stiffening should be between 1/50 and 1/90 of the length of the span.

In the late thirties several bridges were put up in America which went beyond these rules of thumb, and approached the ultimate in slenderness and delicacy of design. One of these was the Bronx-Whitestone bridge, opened in 1939, and designed by O. H. Ammann and Allston Dana. Instead of the open truss stiffening of the deck, it used a continuous plate girder—an idea which had been developed in Germany. The elegance of the bridge with its shallow ribbons of steel in place of a web of truss work was much admired.

On July 1 1940 an even more graceful suspended span opened over the Tacoma Narrows of Puget Sound. At the time, the span of the Tacoma Narrows bridge was the third longest in the world, at 2800 feet. The depth of its plate girder stiffening was only 8 feet (or 1/350 of the span) and the width of roadway only 39 feet (or 1/72 of the span). Even before it was opened, one or two workers on the bridge had felt seasick from its strange undulating behaviour. Once the public got to know of this feature of the bridge, they would come from miles around to enjoy the bizarre roller-coaster car-ride across it. But there seemed to be no doubts about the safety of 'Galloping Gertie' in the public mind—one local bank put up a sign describing itself 'as safe as the Tacoma Bridge'.

On the morning of November 7, barely four months after opening, the oscillations became critical as a 25 to 40 mph wind blew down the Sound. The worried highway authorities stopped traffic over the bridge as sections of the deck began heaving up and down in waves more than three feet high. At 10 o'clock in addition to this vertical motion, the deck began a rhythmic twisting which became steadily more pronounced. Within an hour, the writhing motion had increased in amplitude dramatically, so that, at each wave, one side of the road at each quarter point of the span was 28 feet above the other. At 10.30 a floor panel had broken loose, and at 11.00 a crowd which included press reporters and aghast engineers watched a 600 foot section of the road deck wrench itself from the suspenders and plunge into the Narrows.

The only casualty on that day was a small dog who had been left in a reporter's car when he had abandoned an attempt to drive across the bridge before the collapse. One senior construction engineer, however, had to be restrained by friends from leaping into the Sound after seeing all his work wrecked. The well-known 16mm film of the bridge's fall was shot by Professor F. B. Farquharson of the University of Washington. About a year before, he had carried out some elaborate tests on a model of the bridge to investigate its range of possible harmonic motions. The model had been set in motion by

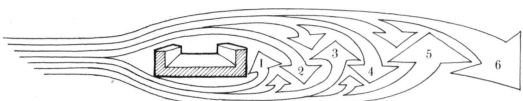

Left *Vortex shedding: a steady wind blowing against an obstruction like a suspended road deck will inevitably cause uneven eddies. These lift and depress the deck alternately.*

123

electro-magnets, not by wind, and although Farquharson had determined the bridge was safe for all the vertical movements, the twisting (or torsional) vibrations which destroyed the bridge had not been foreseen, and consequently not incorporated into the test rig.

New developments

The collapse of the Tacoma Narrows Bridge caused much soul-searching in the civil engineering field and led to some intense research on the dynamic effects of wind on large structures. Other suspension bridges were immediately reviewed. For example, the Bronx-Whitestone was stiffened by a truss added above the plate girder—completely spoiling its outline—and the Golden Gate itself underwent $3 million worth of improvements. It was realized that the problem at Tacoma had been the fact that the shape and extreme flexibility of the bridge made it liable to oscillate. A wind, eddying round the solid face of the stiffening girder, would alternately lift and depress the whole deck. If the wind continued, the oscillating would worsen with the increased momentum of the deck in each cycle. The earlier suspension bridge failures of the Wheeling Bridge and Brown's Brighton Chain Pier were critically re-examined and eyewitness reports were unearthed that described almost identical behaviour, including the twisting. Engineers as a profession had missed the lesson in those cases, although it was the designer of Tacoma Narrows, Leon

University of Washington, and British wind tunnel experiments under the aegis of the Ministry of Transport. The conclusions of all this research produced new formulae and standards for truss-stiffened suspension spans, and several enormous bridges have been built over the last 25 years incorporating them. The main ones are the Mackinac Straits bridge in Michigan (1957), 3800 feet; the Verrazano Narrows, New York (1964), 4260 feet; the Forth Road Bridge (1964), 3300 feet; and the Tagus River Bridge in Lisbon (1966), 3323 feet.

These bridges share most of the necessary features for stable truss-stiffened suspension bridges—deep trusses for rigidity, with both side and cross panels open to allow wind to pass through; vents in the road deck to prevent wind pressure building up too much above or below; and absence of a solid parapet which might create eddies.

The bridge over the Mackinac Straits was the culmination of Steinman's researches in aerodynamics, and was designed with extremely high safety margins, for wind pressure against the superstructure, ice pressure against the piers, and for live loading of the deck. When it was completed in 1957 not only did it boast the world's second longest span (3800 feet) and the world record for total length under cable (8614 feet), but also, was considered by many to be one of the most beautiful suspension bridges ever created. Steinman had, in fact, a reputation for aesthetically pleasing suspension bridges since he designed the attractive St John's Bridge at Portland in Oregon, and the Waldo-Hancock Bridge near Bucksport in Maine, both of which were opened in 1931.

The first proposal to bridge the Verrazano Narrows entrance to New York Harbour was submitted in 1888, but seventy years of discussion and argument over alternative plans followed before work actually started in 1959. The need for an alternative route into New York City from the eastern seaboard states to the south increased as the conurbation spread and population, industry and motor transport grew. In the early days, the objections were largely technical—could such an enormous span actually be built? Later on there were doubts about whether it would be possible to finance such a project. When Steinman and Robinson proposed a 4500 foot span in the late twenties, the War Department vetoed the idea on the grounds that an enemy need only knock the bridge into the Narrows effectively to blockade the Port of New York.

As time passed, the bridge became more and more desperately needed—the War Department changed its views, the necessary legislation was passed and responsibility for the project passed to the Triborough Bridge and Tunnel Authority. The bridge, begun in 1959, was designed by O. H. Ammann (of George Washington fame). Although it was the first bridge for 27 years to take over the world's longest span title from the Golden Gate, the span is only 60 feet longer than

Left above *The Mackinac Bridge, linking the separate peninsulas of the State of Michigan, was opened in 1957, with a main span of 3800 feet and a total of 8614 feet under cable. Its chief designer, D. B. Steinman, incorporated the many refinements and safety improvements resulting from the research that followed the Tacoma collapse.*

Left below *The St John's Bridge at Portland Oregon was built between 1929 and 1931 by Robinson and Steinman.*

Right above *The mighty Verrazano Narrows Bridge links Staten Island directly with Brooklyn across the entrance to New York Harbour. With a main span of 4260 feet, it finally took the record from the Golden Gate Bridge in 1964.*

Moissieff, who had to shoulder most of the blame for the collapse.

David B. Steinman, who probably did more than anyone to increase the understanding of aerodynamic bridge design said:

Once more the elemental forces of nature had conquered—but such victories are only temporary. After each such setback, man proceeds with more perfected knowledge, with greater resourcefulness, and with strengthened resolve, to strive again, to plan again, to build again, to achieve again—all toward renewed triumph and more enduring mastery over the obstacles and destructive forces of nature.

The aftermath of the Tacoma disaster coincided with the Second World War. There were thus reasons why the building of great suspension spans came to a virtual standstill until designs could be formulated to make bridges aerodynamically stable and financial resources could be found for vast engineering projects.

The first suspension bridges built after the war in America tended to be extremely safe, conservative designs well within the rules of thumb. The Tacoma II, for example, 'Gertie's' replacement, was opened in 1950. It is 50 percent heavier than the original and features a comfortably deep 33 feet of Warren truss stiffening. The next generation of bridges, however, was based on the work of Steinman and others, the research at the

the Golden Gate—the height of the towers is in fact some 50 feet less. However, the bridge carries 12 lanes on two levels and the tremendous torsional stiffness of the design permitted a depth of stiffening truss of only 24 feet (1/180 of the span length) producing a graceful profile. Some statistics associated with this project are amazing. For example, the cost amounted to some $320,000,000 of which some $90,000,000 was spent on property, financing and administrative costs. The amount of wire in the cables was enough to encircle the Equator nearly six times. Ammann died in 1965, aged 86, one year after the completion of this, his largest, if not his greatest work.

American expertise in this type of enormous bridge has not been limited to creating spans on American soil. In Lisbon in 1966 a 3323 foot span over the Tagus was opened and christened the 'Ponte Salazar', after the Portuguese dictator. It was constructed by United States Steel International Incorporated, working with the Portuguese government civil engineering department. This again is a large truss-stiffened suspension span which drew on all the lessons of Tacoma— not surprising since the preliminary design was carried out by David Steinman. The structure, which uses an elegant deep Warren truss, is notable as being the only one of these post-war monsters designed to carry a railway in addition to a road. It also boasts the world's deepest foundations—its south pier had to be based on solid rock no less than 240 feet below the river bed.

The eventual challenge to American supremacy in long-span suspension bridges came from Britain. Before the Second World War, plans had been drawn up for a bridge across the estuary of the River Severn, to link the industrial areas of South Wales with southern England. Although the project was shelved during the war, in 1946 discussions were re-started and Mott, Hay and Anderson, and Freeman Fox and Partners were appointed joint consultant engineers. A year later the Ministry of Transport erected a wind tunnel at Thurleigh to carry out experiments on various suspension structures which could be used for the Severn Bridge and a new road bridge over the Firth of Forth. Work on the bridge over the Forth in fact began in 1958, incorporating all the very latest refinements to the design of aerodynamically stable trusses to support the road deck. After work was started, however, a completely different

Below The Forth Road Bridge in Scotland, Britain's greatest truss stiffened suspension span at 3300 feet, was opened by Her Majesty the Queen in 1964. As with the Mackinac Straits Bridge and the Verrazano Narrows Bridge, its design was thoroughly tested in wind tunnel experiments.

easing the load on towers and anchorages, which did not therefore need to be so massive. Fifth, given advances in the technique of welding, the boxes could be pre-fabricated to a large extent. In fact, the 60 foot sections of the deck were made on shore, and with their ends sealed, could be floated out beneath the cables and then lifted into position. The amount of construction work on the bridge itself could be reduced relative to that necessary for truss building. As a final, and incidental bonus, the box section once completed needs less maintenance, since the exterior is smooth and easily painted, and the interior is not exposed to the effects of the weather.

The other departure from conventional suspension bridge design was in the arrangement of the suspenders bearing the weight of the deck from the main cables. In the Severn Bridge, they were placed inclined to one another rather than straight up and down. This feature makes for a more rigid structure.

Work on the foundations for the Severn Bridge began in 1961, and took some two years to complete. Not only is the geology of the site extremely complex (a favourite venue of local geological parties, since so many different kinds of rocks are exposed within a small area), but also

Above *The first box section for the deck of the Severn Bridge is lifted into position. The aerodynamic shape prevents the formation of dangerous eddies and this, combined with the stiffness of the box girder, keeps the deck stable.*

Right *The truss work of the Forth Road Bridge shares a feature common to all truss stiffened suspension spans built since the Second World War—longitudinal vents to allow air through the deck. These prevent the build-up of wind-induced air pressure which could start oscillations.*

structural proposal was put forward by Gilbert Roberts of Freeman Fox and Partners for the construction of the deck of the Severn Bridge. The proposal was based on a new concept of bridge construction that had been evolving since the Second World War. The new concept was the welded box girder.

The revolutionary idea of replacing the trussed suspended deck with a box girder had several clear advantages. First, it saved on the amount of steel. The cross section of the box girder, instead of being very deep, could be very shallow and could be shaped aerodynamically to allow the wind to pass round it smoothly. This second feature reduced both the absolute 'drag' of the deck and lowered the tendency of the deck to create eddies that would make it bounce up and down. Thirdly, the wide hollow section of the box is much better able than a truss to resist the kind of twisting movements that destroyed the first Tacoma bridge. Fourthly, the shallow aerodynamic shape requiring less steel than a truss reduces the dead weight of a long span, thus the range of the tides is around 40 feet and the tidal currents are among the fastest in the country. In 1963, the steel towers were begun, again constructed as hollow boxes. Subsequently, the cables were spun in position, using basically the same technique (standing wires and travelling sheaves carrying a loop of wire) that had been perfected by Roebling. Finally, the deck was suspended, section by section, working from the centre of the span towards each tower.

The Severn Bridge with its 3240 foot main span was officially opened on September 8 1966 and was immediately recognized as a breakthrough in the design of long suspended spans. The firm of Freeman Fox and Partners have since built a longer span using the same principles, over the Bosphorus in Istanbul, Turkey (3524 feet) opened in 1973, and have acted as advisors on other similar projects such as the New Lillebaelt Bridge, Denmark.

The greatest project to make use of the principles of the Severn Bridge is the Humber Bridge, linking the hitherto isolated communities on each side of the Humber estuary on Yorkshire's east coast. The bridge itself will create a new world record span of 4626 feet more than 320 feet longer than the Verrazano Narrows when it is opened. The concrete towers reach 513 feet above sea level which will give a very shallow aesthetic curve to the cables. The Golden Gate towers were 746 feet high, with a consequently deep curve to the cables. However, apart from the great architectural and engineering features of the Humber Bridge, its most important aspect is its place in a general redevelopment scheme for the whole of Humberside, the new administrative region. The bridge over the Humber is another of those works that have been eagerly sought by the local communities, in this case for more than 100 years. The Humberside feasibility study published by the Central Unit for Environmental Planning saw the bridge as the key to opening up industrial and community development in what can now become a new single county. Hull has hitherto been isolated from the south, and Grimsby from the north. The new bridge will cut 40 miles off journeys between the main Humberside centres, and will be the focal point of improved local road systems and co-ordinated schemes for new housing and industry.

Below *The Severn Bridge links the motorways of England and South Wales on a ferry route dating from before the twelfth century. Despite construction problems created by the tides and the geology of the estuary, the streamlined box girder deck enabled great savings to be made on anchorages, towers and cables, to produce the lightest bridge for its size in the world. Chief designer was Sir Gilbert Roberts of Freeman Fox and Partners and the 3240 foot span was opened in 1966.*

Above *When the Humber Bridge is complete it will have the longest span in the world at 4626 feet. As this artist's impression shows, the design will be a scaled up version of the Severn Bridge but with concrete towers and a shallower 'sag' to the cables.*

Left *Work in progress on the Humber Bridge—the foundation pier for the south tower is prepared far offshore in enormous caissons of steel and concrete.*

Concrete

AS A MATERIAL for bridge building, concrete had a less immediate and less spectacular impact than steel. Although engineers took longer to realize its full possibilities, today concrete is everywhere, and is used in a vast array of both bridging and general building applications. Because of its cheapness, weight for weight, it is the chief rival to steel for shorter spans and bridges up to 1000 feet. However, concrete is not a true rival to steel, since modern concrete bridges depend very much on steel, both for reinforcement, and for the tools and technology necessary for construction. The development of concrete bridges has therefore been parallel to developments in steel, and both have been stimulated in the twentieth century by the growth of motor transport and the spread of modern road systems. The main advances in design, however, have not been in the United States, the land of the automobile, but in Europe. Here raw materials have always been scarcer, providing a great need for economical materials. However, the necessary skilled labour is relatively more plentiful, making it feasible to work with this tricky material with time-consuming construction methods.

Basically concrete is a 'conglomerate' of strong but chemically inert aggregates, that is, natural sand and small stones, or artificial mineral materials, bound together by a matrix of mineral cement. Cement hardens and gains strength over a period of time as a result of chemical reactions with water, but, before it hardens, the ingredients for concrete can be mixed into a plastic mass and cast or moulded into virtually any shape. Clearly great care must be taken in the mixing and in the proportions of aggregate to cement and of cement to water. Much research has been carried out to establish the best combinations and to set minimum standards of strength.

The extremely complicated chemical reactions between water, cement and aggregate are still not completely understood, but the resulting product is particularly strong in compression. If steel rods are laid within the concrete mass, it can also be made strong in tension. The other main feature for the bridge builder is the fact that concrete can either be poured into the correct shapes on the bridge itself, or made up at a factory to produce pre-fabricated units. Either way, the engineer had to understand fully, and make allowances for, two odd characteristics of concrete—shrinkage and creep (as well as the temperature-induced changes in size expected in any material). Shrinkage, a slight reduction in volume, occurs as the mixture hardens. The hardening or 'curing' of concrete goes on for such a long time that stresses may build up in the structure, especially when loaded, which can gradually cause deformation of the shape—this is 'creep'.

The secret of the natural cement used by the Romans had virtually disappeared during the Dark Ages and equivalents were not properly re-discovered until the eighteenth century. John Smeaton, for example, was able to use an extremely strong hydraulic mortar to bind the stones of his famous Eddystone Lighthouse, completed in 1759. In 1796, a deposit of natural cement was discovered in the Isle of Sheppey in Kent, and sold as 'Roman Cement' and 'Sheppey stones'. Various other deposits were discovered in Europe and America, but the breakthrough came with the invention of a method of manufacturing cement, by Joseph Aspdin, a Leeds bricklayer. In 1824 he took out a patent for his 'Portland' cement, which he had produced after experiments burning limestone and clay in his kitchen stove. The name 'Portland' was adopted since the finished product resembled in colour and texture the Portland limestone of the Dorset coast—it was not a trade name. By the 1840s, cement was being manufactured on quite a large scale in England, France and Germany. Among the researchers who subsequently developed concrete was François Coignet in France during the 1850s. He was the first to realize the weakening effect of too much water in the concrete mix.

First concrete bridges

The first use of concrete in bridge construction was also in France, when in 1840 a 39 foot solid

Previous page *The Sandö Bridge over the Angerman River in Sweden was built by the Skånska Cement Company between 1937 and 1942. The single rib of 866 feet was cast in situ and the bridge held the record for concrete arches for 30 years.*

Right below *Many early concrete bridges adopted the known structural forms of other materials. The Glenfinnan Viaduct in Inverness was built in 1898 of concrete but it has the appearance of a masonry structure.*

concrete bridge was built over the Garonne Canal at Grisoles. In all the early uses of concrete for bridges, only its great compressive strength was exploited (Stephenson's High Level Bridge at Newcastle, the Eads' bridge at St Louis and Roebling's Brooklyn Bridge all used concrete for foundations). For a while therefore the arch was the only feasible shape for the superstructure of concrete bridges since the arch 'works' only through compression.

One or two such bridges were built in Germany and Switzerland through the 1870s, but it was not until the 1890s that concrete was in general use in bridge superstructures. In the United States, a little 31 foot concrete arch in Brooklyn's Prospect Park was built in 1871 to look as much like stone as possible. The more impressive Glenfinnan Railway viaduct built in Scotland in 1898 also used the arch shapes of its stone-built predecessors.

A French gardener and inventor, Joseph Monier is often credited with the first important work on reinforcing concrete with metal. From 1867 on, he patented a wire mesh system for strengthening many concrete products, including flowerpots, floors and even bridges. However, he was not an engineer and he did little towards establishing how it worked. Far more important were the experiments of the American, W. E. Ward, who in 1871 and 1872 established the need to reinforce the lower, stretched edge of beams. The work of T. Hyatt, published in 1877, took ideas a stage further in working out the relative stresses on the top and bottom surfaces not only of beams, but also of slabs. In many countries, the experiments and experience built up in different ways—in Germany, for example, detailed theories and data on beam and slab design were evolved, while in the United States, Joseph Melan introduced his scheme for arches of steel covered in concrete.

Even with the development of the idea of reinforcing concrete with iron and steel rods, it took a long time for some bridge builders to free themselves of the urge to make concrete bridges look as if they were built of masonry. As late as 1932, for example, the Arlington Memorial Bridge in Washington, D.C., was built not only with eight concrete arches faced with stone, but also with its central bascule span of steel built to match. In 1938, at Wethersfield, Connecticut, the local Highway Department put up a reinforced concrete imitation of a medieval bridge, complete with rough faced 'stone' finish and pointed cutwaters between the traffic lanes. Indeed the

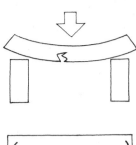

Above *In a beam, bending forces tend to cause cracks in the tension zone where material is stretched. In concrete beams, therefore, reinforcement is best placed near the lower surface, where tension is greatest.*

Above The Arlington Memorial Bridge over the Potomac, Washington D.C. was built in 1932 of reinforced concrete, but it was dressed with a granite facing. The central span is a double leaf bascule in steel, decorated and painted to match the grandiose neo-classical style.

earliest reinforced concrete bridge in America, the 20 foot Alvord Lake Bridge in Golden Gate Park, San Francisco, not only featured imitation rusticated stone voussoirs, but also boasted custom-made cement stalactites dripping from the arch.

Before the turn of the century, the serious work was going on in Europe. From the offices of François Hennebique (1842-1921) in France and Belgium, came a number of textbooks on working with reinforced concrete. Hennebique's improvements to working in concrete included the upward bending of reinforcing bars near supports, and the first use of steel instead of iron. He realized that bridge shapes which were very different from masonry spans were possible in the new material. The most notable of his actual bridges was built in four months for the International Exposition in Liège, Belgium, in 1905. Hennebique designed a 180 foot span across the River Ourthe, with a very flat, thin arch supported at each end on narrow piers. The arch, piers and shorter side-spans were all cast as a continuous structure, and although the crown of the arch was only a foot or so deep, on proving day it took the weight of three steam-rollers.

Robert Maillart

Associated with Hennebique in the first years of this century was a young structural engineer called Robert Maillart (1872-1940). Maillart has since become the most celebrated designer of reinforced concrete bridges, but for much of his career he was so far ahead of his time he was not entrusted with large bridge projects and was often criticized by other engineers.

Maillart was born and educated in Berne, Switzerland and qualified as a structural engineer in 1894. His first professional job was as assistant engineer to the Highways Department of the Zurich City Council, which, when he joined, was considering designs for a steel bridge over the River Sihl. Maillart's alternative flat arch design in reinforced concrete was adopted as its cost would only be some two-thirds that for any steel bridge. The city council subsequently spoiled Maillart's simple plan by adding all kinds of ornamentation—including escutcheons at the crown and decorative pillars on the roadway at each corner. This was typical of the time (1897) when concrete was generally considered as an easy monumental and decorative alternative to stone. It was also typical of Maillart's career. Often his designs were elegant and practical but mistrusted by his clients. They were, however, so cheap that building authorities simply could not afford to ignore them. In 1901 he set up his own firm of contractors, and was soon collaborating with Hennebique on a number of architectural projects. Maillart gained a great deal of experience in using reinforced concrete from this association, but was soon to overtake the older man, especially in the field of bridge design.

The main features which made his bridges such good value were, firstly, the use of the minimum amount of material to carry the loads and secondly, simple, integrated shapes upon which shrinkage, creep, temperature change and foundation movement would have the least possible effect. Maillart rejected many of the standard methods used at the time for computing stresses in concrete, especially those based on Hooke's law which states that the amount of the deformation in an elastic material is proportional to the load placed upon it. He had an uncanny understanding of the more subtle relationships between concrete in its plastic state, its behaviour during hardening, and its final, cured condition. The bridges he designed were thus not only economical, but also aesthetic masterpieces. Artists and architects, at least, admired the rigorous functionalism of his structures even though appreciation from Swiss Canton authorities and the engineering profession took longer.

The shapes Maillart devised were evolved, then, directly from a consideration of concrete as a material, rather than deriving the uses of concrete from the shapes of bridges built in other materials. His two most original forms were the stiffened slab-arch and the three-hinged arch with integral road slabs, both of which 'worked' very differently from previous types of span. Although, of course, the three-hinged arch was not uncommon in steel, the idea had not been considered practical in concrete. In Maillart's bridges, the arch and the girder came together in novel and structurally complex, but visually simple ways.

In 1905, the Tavanasa bridge, the prototype three-hinged arch, was constructed over the River Rhine in Canton Grisons in Switzerland. Over the next 30 years, he refined and extended the form although the basic idea remained the same. Photographs of the bridge (it was destroyed in a land-slide in 1927), show it to have looked, even by today's standards, remarkably modern. At each abutment, the 167 foot arch began as a pair

of 'legs', which thickened and fused towards quarter span. At this point also the arches joined the road slab, itself a structural element of the bridge obviating the need for spandrel support. Over the central section of the bridge, the deck, the walls and the arch came together to form a hollow box section—a unified, continuous shape, (except at the central hinge), made possible by being able to pour fresh concrete into moulds. The forces in the structure were concentrated on the three hinges, at the abutments and at the crown. Although these hinges were concrete, and strongly reinforced, their relative flexibility did allow slight shrinkage, creep and temperature-induced movements of the bridge.

In the Tavanasa, as in all Maillart's bridges, enormous care went into the position and quantity of the steel reinforcing rods to obtain their maximum effect. Since Maillart was committed to the idea of minimum materials, the reinforcing was critically important. Another reason for extreme care is that cracks tend to appear in concrete in any tension zone. Thus, the more effective the reinforcement, the smaller these cracks will be, keeping the bridge strong and the embedded steel itself protected from the atmosphere.

Stiffened slab-arch

Maillart's improvements on his three-hinged arch at Tavanasa came with some of the longer spans he was commissioned to carry out in later life. The

Below Waterloo Bridge over the Thames replaced Rennie's original structure in 1945 with a continuous concrete beam with five 240 foot spans. Despite the pleasing arch shape of the spans, the portland stone dressing was laid vertically to avoid the misleading impression of a voussoir arch.

later bridges were built without the rather
ponderous abutments, and the continuous road
deck slab was supported on thin vertical walls,
making his bridges more elegant still. His most
spectacular bridge of this type was the Salinga-
tobel Bridge over a deep mountain gorge near
Schiers (in Switzerland). It was constructed
between 1929 and 1930 with a 292 foot three-
hinged arch, and an overall length of 432 feet. It
could only have been built in Switzerland; not
only was there Maillart himself, but for the
prodigious problems of erecting the scaffolding
supports, there were Swiss craftsmen (in this case
the Coray family of Chur) specializing in that type
of false work.

The other major innovation introduced by
Maillart in reinforced concrete bridge construction
was the stiffened slab-arch. These bridges have a
rigid, heavy deck slab, which is supported on an
extremely thin arched slab, via even thinner
transverse vertical walls. The rigidity of the deck
slab is important in two ways. Since the deck is
joined firmly to the arch at its crown, and
anchored firmly at its ends, the deck's horizontal
strength (along the roadway) restricts any lateral
movement in the arch and thus prevents it from
changing its shape. Secondly, the deck slab's
stiffness will tend to distribute local loads over
the whole length of the arch, so that buckling in
the arch is prevented.

In 1933 Maillart and W. Pfeiffer constructed a
footbridge near Wulflingen, Zurich. It has a span
of 124 feet, yet the concrete at the crown of the
arch is only $4\frac{1}{2}$ inches thick. More notable is the
Schwandbach Bridge, in Canton Berne, carrying
the highway 111 feet over a gorge. The vault of
the arch is 7.9 inches, and the crosswalls 6.3

inches thick. Further, the whole bridge is actually
built on a curve—the inner edge of the arch vault
follows the curve of the road deck and the outer
edge is built straight across the valley, so it can
withstand, via the angled edges of the crosswalls,
centrifugal forces set up by motor traffic going
round the bend.

Mainstream design

While Maillart used reinforced concrete in these
extremely original ways, the mainstream of
bridge design in this material was more conservative. It was concerned with exploiting
concrete's massive strength in compression using
more ordinary arch forms. Some of these, however, were very impressive, and by the 1930s and
1940s, the technology of concrete arches had
advanced enough to produce some fine, delicate
structures. Early on, however, concrete bridges
tended to be ponderous.

One of the most massive of the early bridges to
use reinforced concrete arches was the Tunkhannock Viaduct in Pennsylvania, built in 1916 to
shorten one of the railway routes into New York.
Ten 180 foot arches carry a double track railway
line half a mile over the valley of Tunkhannock
Creek. For its 240 foot high piers, with each deck
supported on ten solid crosswalls from the thick
arch vaults, some 167,000 cubic yards of concrete
were used.

As time passed and the lighter loads of road
traffic replaced the heavyweight demands of the
railways, engineers learnt to save material; heavy
abutments and piers were not really necessary
with concrete arches since the thrusts of the
vaults were concentrated at the foundations. The

open spandrels, of course, exerted no horizontal thrust. Gradually too, the supporting walls for decks became lighter and lighter, and slim posts were sometimes used in their stead. The arch-vaults themselves became thinner, and as with medieval builders, ribbed arches made further savings possible.

Several bridges may be quoted by way of illustration: Royal Tweed Bridge (1928) at Berwick in Scotland, the Gueroz Bridge (1933) over the Trient Valley, Valais in Switzerland, the Traneberg Bridge (1934) over a section of Stock-holm Harbour in Sweden, and the Sandö Bridge (1942) across the River Angerman along the border of Norway and Sweden.

The Sandöbron between Norway and Sweden was, until 1963, the world's longest concrete span (866 feet). It has been said that the thin concrete posts were closer to steel design in their treatment. In fact, several types of bridge usually built in steel were tried in concrete, including trusses, tied arches and through arches. Of these, the through arch was the most successful—several were built in Sweden by the Skånska Cement Company, but the two best examples were constructed in France over the Seine and both were destroyed in the Second World War. These were the La Roche-Guyon Bridge (1934) with a span of 528 feet, and the St Pierre de Vouvray Bridge of 430 feet built in 1922. The latter, when it was built, was a record span in concrete, but even more remarkable was the fact that the twin ribs were braced together in two places only—over the roadway at each end.

Pre-stressed concrete

The designer of this bridge was Eugène Freyssinet (1879-1962) who made enormous contributions to the ideas and practice of bridge making in concrete. Like Maillart, he was not satisfied with the inadequate and highly theoretical approaches to bridge building, especially those favoured by the *Ecole des Ponts et Chausées*, where he studied. He once wrote:

Centre The Schwandbach Bridge was constructed in 1933 and was an ingenious curved variation on Maillart's stiffened slab arch technique. Like many of his bridges, the design was considered too daring to use for anything more important than a local road.

Below The Tunkhannock Viaduct dates from 1915—the era of monumental American bridges like the Hell Gate arch and the Sciotoville truss. Ten concrete arches carry the railroad for nearly half a mile, 240 feet above the Tunkhannock Creek valley in Pennsylvania.

It has been said that it was the Freyssinet family's peasant background that lay behind the engineer's particularly direct and practical approach to bridging problems.

The most important of Freyssinet's contributions was his development of the concept of prestressing, which he thought up about 1904, although it took some 20 years to bring to full practicability. In ordinary reinforced concrete, the cement and aggregate mixture is poured into forms or moulds, around the reinforcing rods and bars. As the concrete is hardening, the formwork bears the loading. Not until the forms are removed does the concrete come under any stress. This is the stage when loading, combined with shrinkage, vibration and temperature change, does most damage, and cracks appear in zones of tension. Freyssinet's idea was to induce into the concrete before erection, stresses that would counteract those in the finished structure. Given an accurate computation of these stresses, dead weight could effectively be ignored in the finished span since the stresses it produced had already been catered for during manufacture and erection. This process would provide, in his own words, *resultant stresses which are limited to values that can be sustained indefinitely by the materials, without the latter suffering by change.*

Two methods of pre-stressing were evolved which are still standard practice. Concrete can be poured into moulds through which run steel wires or rods held in tension until the concrete has hardened. Then the ends of the steel are released, but the solid concrete holds it in tension. This produces a pre-tensioned member. Alternatively, the member can be cast without the steel, but with holes or ducts running through it. When the concrete has cured, cables or bars are laid through the holes, stretched and then sealed ('grouted') in the beam with cement. This produces a post-tensioned member. In either method, Freyssinet realized the tensioned reinforcement had to be high-tensile steel. It would have to be stretched beyond its eventual, designed tension, since in the process of drying out the concrete would shrink, and tend to lessen the effect of the embedded steel. Also, ordinary mild steel could not be used since it could simply not be stretched far enough before yielding.

The implications of Freyssinet's techniques have been enormous, and have led to pre-stressed concrete being used for vast numbers of the short and medium spans necessary in the construction of modern motorways. Pre-stressing meant that beams, slabs, voussoirs and so on, could be mass-produced under factory conditions and not necessarily cast on site. Quality could be more easily controlled, while at the same time the cost would be kept down, both from economies of scale and from reducing the need for complex formwork and scaffolding. Pre-cast units could be joined on site by stringing them together with high tensile steel rods or cables to produce a complete pre-stressed structure. Such construction used at least 70 percent less steel and between 30 and 40 percent less concrete than ordinary reinforced concrete.

Pre-stressing thus produced a strong material from relatively little steel and concrete, although the material itself is an expensive one to manufacture. The design advantages, however, were so considerable that the technique was bound to have an effect on the actual shapes of bridges.

Before the Second World War, Freyssinet's main work was with arches. In addition to his St Pierre de Vouvray Bridge mentioned earlier, he designed the three-arch Plougastel Bridge over the Elorn River near Brest. It was completed in 1930, with spans about 600 feet. Freyssinet had each arch cast on centering which could be floated out on barges when the arch was finished. For this bridge he also invented and developed a technique of building jacks into the structure, which were used to spring the arch off the formwork, and to correct any slight deformations in the arch shape. With the arch trimmed up, the oil in the jacks was replaced with cement to make them permanent fixtures.

Freyssinet was a great concrete arch enthusiast. He submitted a 3281 foot proposal for the Hudson crossing in 1928, and he acted as consultant on several large concrete spans, including the Traneberg arch. However, during and after the Second World War, his pre-stressing work led him to devise a novel form of bridge: this was the portal frame. In principle, the vertical posts which support each end of a beam are made as part of that beam. A proportion of the bending effects on the beam can be taken up by stressing the base of the end supports inwards. Thus, a greater span can be achieved than with a straightforward beam. Put another way, for the same span, the frame bridge can be much more slender than a beam. The frame also has an advantage over the arch in that, for navigable waters, the bridge does not have to be constructed so high to achieve a satisfactory channel with adequate clearance.

In France, after the Second World War, many bridges destroyed in the fighting needed replacing. Among them were five crossings over the River

Left above *The inclined roadway over the progressively larger spans of the Royal Tweed Bridge at Berwick was opened in 1928. The separate ribs and the open spandrel supports over the piers emphasize the way the concrete structure 'works'.*

Left centre *A younger contemporary of Maillart's, A. Sarrasin, built the Gueroz Bridge in Canton Valais, Switzerland, between 1931 and 1933. The roadway is supported by an integrated combination of the slender arch ribs with the solid parapets—a clear span of 323 feet.*

Left below *Freyssinet's 430 foot reinforced concrete span over the River Seine at St Pierre du Vouvray was completed in 1922. He proposed in 1928 a similar 3281 foot structure to cross the Hudson River.*

Right above *Eugène Freyssinet was one of the world's foremost designers of concrete bridges. One of his many important structures in France was the Plougastel Bridge over the River Elorn, which was opened in 1930.*

139

Above *The bridge over the River Marne at Annet was one of the five identical pre-stressed concrete spans that Freyssinet developed after the Second World War from a prototype at Luzancy. The three slender ribs of each 240 foot span were constructed (between 1948 and 1950) by stressing pre-cast sections together with high tensile steel cable.*

Marne, at Esbly, Annet, Tribardou, Changis and Ussey and Freyssinet's pre-stressed frame units were used to construct novel bridges in each location. The 180 foot prototype at Luzancy had in fact been started in 1941 but had been held up in the hostilities, and was completed in 1946. Based on this structure, Freyssinet designed the five bridges all identical with 240 foot spans. The concrete parts for all the bridges could thus be batch produced. The plan was ideal for the difficult economic climate, the bridges were cheap, they used relatively little steel—very scarce at the time—and were quick to construct, needing no elaborate falsework or moulds for on-site casting.

The six ribs for each bridge were made up of short, pre-cast I-beam voussoirs, six of which were stressed together to form the three main parts of each rib. At the site, the portal legs were first placed at the abutments. Then the central sections added and all three parts pulled together with longitudinal high tension cables. Finally, the ribs were stressed to each other with transverse rods. The other important pre-stressing was vertical pre-tensioning through the four-inch thick web of each voussoir, to counteract the very high sheer forces which would otherwise lead to diagonal cracks appearing.

Motorways and viaducts

Freyssinet of course was not the only one to use pre-stressed concrete, although he was, perhaps, the greatest pioneer in the field. Since the Second World War especially, the ideas and techniques of pre-stressing have been developed and refined in many ways, for improved kinds of bridges in many locations around the world. Large motorway projects especially have required the application of the basic concrete technology to produce the large variety of necessary spans. The motorway itself has to be carried, not only over the natural obstacles of river valleys and such like

but also over, rather than through, whole sections of the urban environment. For such elevated roads, massive cantilevers of enormous strength have been evolved. For bridges carrying farm tracks, minor roads, footpaths or even other motorways over the main route, a great array of beams, cantilevers, portal frames and arches are now used.

It is now universally recognized that good bridge design, especially in concrete, has nothing to do with embellishment, or even symmetry. It is also recognized now that the psychological effects of motorway bridges are important for drivers. Several early German autobahns featured acommodation bridges with straight, powerful concrete girders which drivers considered psychological obstructions to high speed motoring. The beam bridges of the first section of Britain's M1 motorway create the same effect—aggravated by the fact that they look virtually identical and provide none of the badly needed mental relief for long distance motorway travel. More modern motorway bridges are thus lighter, more interesting structurally, and more varied.

One of the most useful of the post-war developments of concrete bridge construction stimulated by motorway spread, has been the hollow concrete box girder. Among the finest examples of this type is the bridge which carries the M2 over the River Medway in Kent. Many principles came together in this bridge—the work of Stephenson and Fairbairn on box-sections for the Britannia Bridge; the balanced cantilever construction of Baker and Fowlers Forth Bridge; and, tying it all together, the techniques of pre-stressing concrete evolved by Freyssinet and others like the Belgian, Gustav Mangel. The main span of the Medway bridge is 500 feet with cantilevers supporting a 200 foot suspended beam. The cantilevers were built out one section at a time, from either side of the thin slab walls, forming the piers. Each extra addition to the cantilever arms, had to be exactly balanced by the next unit being added to the arm on the other side of the pier. The cantilevering technique in concrete had been pioneered in 1952 in a bridge over the Rhine at Worms.

Long distance bridges

Apart from motorway bridges, concrete had been used in most of the world's longest overall bridge systems. Henry Flager's Key West extension in 1912 joined Key West, 37 miles off the end of Florida, with the mainland. It contained 20 miles of embankments, 38 individual steel and concrete bridges, three drawbridges and 29 concrete viaducts, nearly all of them across the open, but shallow sea. For years the 2.15 mile Long Key Viaduct was the longest open water crossing in the world, but apart from the staggering overall length of the system, and the formidable logistics of construction, there was little of structural interest in the bridges. Later came the $17\frac{1}{2}$ miles of the Chesapeake Bay bridge and tunnel combination, 12 miles of which were low-level concrete trestles. More distinguished is the Oosterschelde Bridge, a three mile link between Rotterdam and south-west Holland, opened in 1966. Its 48 identical spans, each 312 feet, are pre-stressed concrete cantilevers. For these long bridges, the economic advantages of concrete, especially when standardized pre-cast units or formwork are used, are even more pronounced when taking into account the low maintenance costs of concrete once the bridge is complete.

Left The Gravelly Hill motorway interchange near Birmingham, England, demonstrates the association of bridge making in concrete with the growth of road transport. Such vast schemes, although feats of engineering ingenuity, are not always a direct benefit to neighbouring communities.

Below The main cantilevers of the M2 motorway Medway Bridge shown under construction. Steel towers below the anchor spans were used to help maintain the precise balance of the arms as more hollow concrete box sections were added to each end.

Perhaps the most interesting of the long viaducts, however, is the five mile bridge across Lake Maracaibo in Venezuela, linking the oil country on the eastern lake shore with Maracaibo, the capital of the state of Zulia. The bridge became a necessity during the 1950s, when ferry services started to become inadequate for the traffic generated by oil development. The bridge was based on designs by Professor Riccardo Morandi, although a huge number of contractors, structural analysts, geologists and planners was assembled from Germany, Switzerland, Portugal, France and Venezuela to turn the plans into a reality. Much of the detailed planning work revolved around how to make the best use of standardized units both of pre-cast concrete girders and of re-usable steel forms for *in situ* casting.

The approaches to the main spans are carried on original V and H shaped piers with double cantilevers integrally cast on top of each prong. The main interest of the bridge however is in the five central spans each of 780 feet. The structural unit is not the span itself, but each pier, which has a double-ended cantilever deck 616 feet long supported by heavy cables from the central tower. The cable stays enable the cantilever arms to be considerably long without being correspondingly deep, and without needing a massive amount of reinforcement. Overall, the way these units 'work' is generally similar to that of the Forth Bridge.

Each unit of the bridge is linked to the next with a pre-cast 'fish belly' girder, thicker in the middle, the zone of greatest stress, than at each end. Each beam is fixed at one end, and free to move on steel-sheathed concrete rollers at the other. Thus, each section of the bridge is quite independent of the next, an oddity in these days of continuous structures. The reason, however, lies in the Maracaibo area's susceptibility to earthquakes. In a continuous structure, damage to one part would weaken the entire bridge. With each section independent, however, collapse of one section would leave its neighbour unaffected.

Although an army of consultants and constructors worked on the project, Morandi's influence was very strong. His distinctive ideas can be seen in his other design projects for the Göteborg Harbour Bridge in Sweden, the Polcevera Creek Bridge in the Genoa-Savona Autostrada in Italy and the Columbia River Bridge at Kinnaird in Canada. All these examples indicate the general trend in large bridge projects towards international collaboration between designers, construction companies and even governments. The Maracaibo Lake Bridge in particular, highlights the shift in the world's attention from the older-established communities towards countries of the Third World.

With the improvements in concrete bridge construction and design being made all the time, it is interesting that one of the most advanced spans in recent years has used the age-old technique of a voussoir arch erected on falsework. This is the Australian Gladesville Bridge, opened

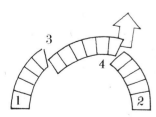

in 1964, across the Parramatta River near the great Sydney Harbour Bridge. Since the last serious users of this method in the nineteenth century, however, there had been great advances in the understanding of the behaviour of voussoir arches, particularly in the effects of uneven loads, of spread between abutments and of buckling. Also, a great deal of work had been done specifically on concrete in arches and the problems of rib-shortening from shrinkage or from 'settling' under the enormous compression forces in long concrete spans. Generally it was realized that an arch would fail when it became a four-hinged mechanism—when the combination of ribs shortening, abutments spreading and loading being uneven, caused too much bending in the arch ring. The danger would occur when uneven compressions in the arch would shift the main lines of thrust too far from the centre line of the voussoirs.

The Gladesville arch was to be made up of hollow concrete boxes varying in size between 20 by 22 by 11 feet at the abutments, and 20 by 14 by 7½ feet at the crown. Four ribs of these voussoirs were joined by their extended top flanges to form the arch. The pre-cast voussoirs were made on shore, fully cured, then hoisted on to the steel falsework and cemented against their neighbours. About five to six units were placed each day. The centering itself was an elaborate construction in tubular steel, with a 220 foot truss on one side to allow the waterway to stay open to shipping while the bridge was being built. Eugène Freyssinet was one of the consultants on this bridge, and many of his techniques were used, including that developed at Plougastel for springing the arch from the centering and straightening it up by jacks to correct any shrinkage and creep in the cement joints; effects that could have shortened the ribs.

With its 1000 foot span, the bridge is so large that its own dead weight is by far the greatest part of the total loading, so the distribution of the weight of the roadway deck was the most important consideration in preventing any uneven bending forces on the arch itself. Although the shape of the bridge appears very simple, a most sophisticated series of crosswalls, diaphragms and hinges had to be used in the construction of the deck and its integration with the piers and the arch.

With this bridge and two 1100 foot spans—at Mesopotamia, Brazil and Georges River, Australia —we see how concrete is being used for larger and larger spans. More important however, is its versatility. Some of the most interesting concrete bridges are the smallest footbridges which allow the designer to create structures for light live loads without the necessity for a corresponding large dead load. Ove Arup's Kingsgate Bridge in Durham is perhaps the finest example, which uses the absolute minimum of material in a continuous U shaped girder footway, supported on slim braced V piers.

New Shapes
in Steel

SINCE THE SECOND World War, the shape of European bridge building in steel has been dominated by one structural concept—the box girder. The technology of materials and construction techniques finally caught up with the pioneering ideas of Stephenson and Fairbairn and the Britannia tubular bridge, to produce the only really economical alternative to concrete. Although the box girder principle is equally important in concrete bridge design, it is with steel that the idea has achieved the greatest variety and elegance. Whether as a simple beam, a cantilever, a cable stayed deck, or forming the roadway for the longest suspension bridge, the steel box girder is undeniably the bridge form of the present day. These bridges are on the 'growing edge' of technology, using concepts similar to those in aircraft and ship design, and the most modern methods of construction from automated welding to structural analysis with electronic computers. Despite their sophistication, however, steel box girders have shared with suspension bridges the fate of discovering their limiting factors through disaster.

Among the first modern bridges to use the box girder principle were, in fact, several concrete spans like London's Waterloo Bridge, opened in 1942. Work in steel, however, began with the development of beam bridges using two or more continuous I-beams or plate girders to support a steel deck. The development of welding techniques was important here, both for the joining of the girder webs to form a continuous beam, and in the joining of the girder flanges to the deck. Developments in welding methods were forced during the Second World War in the ship building industry, where several welded steel ships broke in half and the concept of 'brittle fracture' at low temperatures evolved.

However, the 'plate girder' bridges were not capable of long spans, because, as in any beam structure, with longer spans the depth of the girders soon became prohibitive. More important, it was realized that long parallel I-beams were liable to buckling in their vertical webs unless joined together transversely at frequent intervals. One answer to this problem was to make the webs themselves thicker and thus stiffer. The disadvantage of this solution was that the amount of steel necessary for the extra stiffening made the beams both heavier, and unnecessarily strong for a given span. The steel was not used to its best advantage; it worked at levels well below its maximum permissable stress.

The other solution to the buckling problem was to make the join between the flanges of the girders continuous—to form, in fact, a hollow box. In this way, the depth of the girder can be reduced and a considerable amount of steel may be saved. The bridge designer is thus able to work much closer to the permissable stress of his material. The box section shape provides great strength using thin steel sheet; as might be expected with such thin material, buckling again becomes a serious danger. Clearly, buckling of any face of the box would destroy the shape and lead to failure, so the box-section is maintained by longitudinal 'stringers' (stiffeners inside each face), and lateral bulkheads.

Along with the evolution of this idea, and of the technique of welding, two other factors were important in the 1940s and 1950s. The first was the lack of an economic building method for spans up to 1500 feet. Over that length the suspension bridge comes into its own. Below that length, suspension spans not only are relatively expensive to erect, but also their critical requirements for suitable anchorages and for tower

Previous page The Rio-Niteroi Bridge under construction in 1973, across Guanabara Bay, Brazil. Steel box girders make up the three central spans which had to have high enough clearance for sea navigation and no towers to obstruct aircraft. The 900 foot sidespan units were constructed on shore, floated out, and jacked, complete to the tops of the piers.

Left below One of the six continuous box girder spans of the Europe Bridge on the Bremer Pass near Innsbruck, Austria. The roadway of the 600 foot main span is 624 feet above the valley and was, until recently, the highest in Europe.

Right above and centre The trussed Auckland Harbour Bridge in New Zealand was opened in 1959 (above). By 1964, however, traffic had increased so much that it became necessary to double the bridge's capacity. The two continuous box girders that were added to the existing structure (centre) demonstrate the aesthetic advantages and the reduction in structural depth possible with the new technique.

Below *The first modern box girders were evolved by joining the flanges of parallel I-beams. Since then a variety of configurations have been developed for different or special circumstances.*

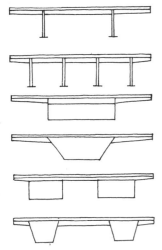

foundations rule out many sites. Also, small suspension spans may be liable to instability under live loading. The second factor was the Second World War, which had left so many European bridges in ruins and which, as we have seen, also stimulated the use of pre-stressed concrete. The majority of important spans needing reconstruction were in this medium to long-span range, and the first steel box girders were built in Germany where the devastation was greatest.

The advantages of this type of bridge are clear. Since box sections only need to be relatively shallow, high approaches are not always necessary. They offer a strong, light structure which can make best use of scarce steel. Their lightness means that many of the structural parts can be prefabricated and transported to the site. Once there, the bridge can be put up either by launching individual sections off, or hauling them up on to those already erected. Alternatively, several boxes can be joined at ground level and lifted into position all together. Once erected, the top surface of the box-sections provides a ready-made deck to lay concrete or road surfacing. Further, the shape of box girders makes them very strong in

resisting torsional stresses—for example, the twisting action of uneven traffic loadings on one side of the deck. Later on, it was realized that box-sections could be shaped with an aerodynamic cross-section, giving them the added advantage of being better able to withstand wind loading. Finally, box bridges look so simple and uncluttered, they can have considerable aesthetic appeal.

The box girder is not a single type of bridge, so much as a principle which can be used in a number of ways. For short spans, or for approach viaducts which require a large number of short spans, box girders can make up a straightforward continuous beam. In this sort of range, however, the competition from concrete is fairly stiff. For spans up to about 750 feet, the beam can be thickened over the piers to form a cantilever—usually built continuous with the approach viaduct; sometimes, a central span will be long enough to warrant a suspended beam. As an alternative to the cantilever, and for spans up to 1500 feet, the beam can be cable-stayed for additional support.

The box girder principle has been used in a

great many European bridges. Some have used a number of fairly small girders to hold up a wide deck; for example, the Opelkriesel flyover in Frankfurt-am-Main or the Moat Street flyover in Coventry—both parts of elaborate urban road schemes. More recently, for motorway crossings of large natural obstacles, bigger twin boxes have been used, as for example, in the M5 crossing at Avonmouth. The 132 foot wide deck forms the top flange of twin parallel boxes, 19 feet 6 inches wide and 10 feet deep for the approach viaduct beams and 25 feet deep over the piers at either end of the main span of 570 feet. The continuous beam with these slight variations in girder depth forms a bridge of great elegance and simplicity.

Rio Niteroi Bridge

The most spectacular of these continuous beam and cantilever combinations is the central section of the Rio-Niteroi bridge in Brazil. For such a long bridge (5 miles over water), the most economical material for most of its length was of course concrete, and some 3000 261-foot concrete boxes form the approaches to the navigation channels. The clearance required for shipping was nearly 200 feet of headroom over a 930 foot wide channel. At the same time, aviation demands from the nearby Santos Dumont airport meant that no part of the structure could be more than 240 feet high. A steel twin box girder was thus the only realistic possibility, for this length and slenderness of span.

Steel parts for the central section were made in Britain and shipped to South America, where they were welded up into three enormous pairs of boxes in a special construction yard near the bridge site. The 606 foot long suspended span was built to be used first as a pontoon for floating out the larger side-span units. The side-span units, 945 feet and weighing 2250 tonnes, were jacked in pairs on to their concrete towers. The sidespans had a 96 foot cantilever towards the approach viaduct and a 201 foot projection over the main navigation channel. The channel span was completed by hoisting the suspended (pontoon) beam into position between the side-span cantilevers.

The organizations involved in constructing the bridge included the British Redpath Dorman Long Limited and the Cleveland Bridge and Engineering Company Limited, working with the Brazilian firm of Montreal Engenharia SA; consulting engineers were Needles, Tammen and Bergendoff International, USA, and the whole project developed for Brazil's Departamento Nacional de Estradas de Rodagem, the Highway Department of the Ministry of Transport. Like Maracaibo Bridge, the project demonstrates the international approach to bridge building in developing countries, where the greatest challenges are nowadays to be found. The Rio-Niteroi Bridge is very important in the general development of Brazil, forming as it does, the last link in the 2500 mile road system linking north and south Brazil along the coast. It was opened in 1974 and given its

Above and right The clean sweep of the Avonmouth Bridge carries the M5 motorway into South-West England. The 132 foot wide roadway is carried on two parallel box sections (under construction, right) joined by conventional steel girders and resting on pairs of concrete pillars. Note the stiffening battens inside the box section to prevent buckling.

official name, Ponte Presidente Costa e Silva.

Its long span, however, was only possible with a deep box section at each end. In some locations, this depth of girder can be a disadvantage. For example, where high approaches are not possible, this extra depth may seriously limit headroom. One of the previous record holders for long span girders was the 856 foot span of the Sava Bridge in Belgrade, which required a structural depth over the piers of 32 feet. Where conditions permit, the technique that is now used for this range of span is the cable stayed box girder. This method, which evolved simultaneously with plain box girders, involves using a continuous box of constant depth with support from radial stays slung from towers at the piers. The stays act in place of extra piers and allow for a long span to be achieved with a reduced amount of steel in the box girder itself.

Cable stayed bridges

An early attempt at a stayed bridge was the Albert Bridge, built in 1873 over the River Thames in London. This however was a hybrid structure, part cantilever, part suspension and part stayed bridge using wrought iron flats. The first modern cable stayed bridge was a 600 foot span constructed by German engineers at Strömsund in Sweden in 1956. Thereafter Germany led the field in developing this type of bridge.

All the early cable stayed bridges used the two plane system with cables from twin towers supporting both edges of the deck. The Theodore Hauss bridge (1958) in Düsseldorf—main span 849 feet—and the Rhine Bridge at Rees are examples of this type, both using a number of parallel cables from the four towers, known as 'harp' construction. The Severins Bridge at Cologne (1959) employs five pairs of radial stays supported from a giant A-frame 196 feet high, to support two asymmetric spans of 395 feet and 987 feet.

However, as box girders developed, it became possible to utilize their great torsional strength to allow the support of the deck with single-plane stays rigged between single towers and points within the central reservation of the roadway. The support for these cables is transmitted to the whole width of the deck via stiff transverse crossbeams. Visually single-plane cables are simpler and less fussy than two planes. One of the problems with the two-plane system had been whether to anchor the cables inside or beyond the extreme edges of the deck.

The prototype single plane cable stayed bridge was the Norderelbe Bridge in Hamburg, completed in 1962. The deck consists of a wide stiffened steel plate supported on a central rectangular box girder and an outside pair of plate girders. Although the side spans were constructed on staging, the main span girders were cantilevered out from each pier 185 feet before needing the support of guy ropes from the towers. When the two cantilevers met at mid-span, the cables were rigged and tensioned to take the load of the main span.

For a cable stayed bridge to work properly, the cables themselves have to be extremely powerful and must act on the deck with as much rigidity as an intermediate pier would. Several of the early attempts to build cable stayed bridges were not successful since the cables used stretched too much to be able to provide the vertical support necessary. The modern answer to this problem is the 'locked coil' cable, in which coils of specially formulated steel are combined in a way that restricts the tendency to unwind which is found in conventionally spun cables.

After the Norderelbe bridge, the next important step within a few years was the refinement of the deck itself, to a trapezoidal cross-section. While the most well known application of this aerodynamic idea is in the long suspension bridges, it is also important in beam and cable stayed spans. The trapezoidal box girder first made its appearance in a fairly small span (324 feet)—Julicher Strasse, over a marshalling yard in Düsseldorf—but more impressive was the Leverkusen Bridge with a 280 foot main span.

The other refinement with this type of bridge is in the arrangement of the cables. Although the trapezoidal box girder is now virtually standard in cable stayed spans, the cable pattern may vary a great deal. At one end of the scale are the twenty strings of the 'Rheinharf' (or the Heidrich Ebert Bridge) in Bonn, while at the other are the severely economical single cables of the Wye Bridge and the Erskine Bridge in Britain. The Wye Viaduct which was opened in 1966, carries the M4 into Wales from the end of the great Severn Suspension Bridge. Because of its nearness to the larger span, the Wye Bridge has largely been overlooked despite its 770 foot span and the fact that it was Britain's first single plane cable stayed bridge. From the Wye Bridge was developed what is currently the most fabulously light and simple of the cable stayed bridges—the Erskine Bridge near Glasgow. The main span of the Erskine (opened in 1974) carries a section of the M898 1000 feet over the Clyde estuary. For nearly a mile, the motorway runs on a continuous trapezoidal box girder, similar to that used in the Severn and Humber bridge road decks, itself supported on the slimmest concrete piers.

The failure of box girders

The evolution of steel box girders, however, has not been a trouble-free progress towards their present highly sophisticated form. One of their most serious problems has been the fact that, during erection, as box sections are progressively cantilevered out, the stresses within the beams become more acute. Over the piers, these stresses are often several times the eventual load in the completed span. The deflection of the cantilevered sections may be very pronounced—for example, the ends of each half of the main span of the Wye

bridge had to be jacked up some 10 feet to meet and form the continuous deck.

In 1970, the world's attention was focused on steel box girder construction when, within a short time, four bridges of this type collapsed as they were being built. The four bridges were in Vienna, over the Danube, in Milford Haven, Wales, where four men were killed, in Melbourne over the Lower Yarra River and another Rhine Bridge in Germany. By far the most serious of these was the fall of the West Gate Bridge in Melbourne. It was being built on the same principle as the Wye Bridge, to be a cable stayed continuous beam with a 1102 foot main span. On October 15 1970 the west cantilevered section, by then 376 feet 6 inches long and weighing 1200 tons, crashed 160 feet from its pier on to huts where many workmen were having their lunch. Thirty five men lost their lives, including the resident engineer. Many more were injured and rescue operations were seriously hampered by mud and fires from spilt diesel oil.

The immediate cause of the collapse appears to have been a serious buckle which had developed in the central plate joining the two halves of the box girders. To make construction easier, each complete box section was prefabricated in separate halves, hoisted into position and bolted together. A serious mis-match had occurred between the halves of the west cantilever section and some 60 tons of concrete ballast had been placed on the higher section to deflect it the $4\frac{1}{2}$ inches necessary to make the join. The alternative would have been a time-consuming and thus expensive jacking operation. The buckle which had appeared as a result of this procedure was, in fact, being investigated when the bridge fell.

Two construction companies were involved in the day to day erection operations, the local John Holland and Company and a Dutch firm, World

Services and Construction. The story is really about the complexities of the relations between them and the other organizations involved in the project; the designing engineers, Freeman Fox and Partners, the consultant engineers, Mansell and Partners of Melbourne, The Lower Yarra Crossing Authority and, of course, the workers themselves and their unions. The confused situation that led to the disaster was investigated at an inquiry set up under Mr Justice Barber of the New South Wales Supreme Court. The report of the inquiry concluded:

While we have found it necessary to make some criticism of all the other parties, justice to them requires us to state unequivocally that the greater part of the blame must be attributed to Freeman Fox and Partners.

Since the West Gate failure followed the Milford Haven collapse by just four months, the British Government immediately set up a committee, chaired by Dr Merrison, to investigate as a matter of urgency, the bridge failures, the rules for appraising structures during building, and the basic technical standards of construction methods and materials. In the meantime a mass of short and long-term research was begun, and in Britain traffic was immediately restricted on completed box girder bridges, some of which had been in operation for several years.

What has emerged is that the box girder concept is fundamentally sound and that standards and specifications in both design and fabrication are acceptable, with a number of modifications. What had not been adequate were the methods and routines for checking that design standards and specifications were being met in the fabrication. In the general quest for the most economic structure the proper organization of these expensive confirmation procedures had tended to be overlooked. The revised rules for box girder construction as set out in the Merrison Report, published in 1973, have meant that bridges completed since, have been rather more costly because of the necessary checking procedures. As one engineer put it: *The difficulty is not achieving the Merrison standards but in proving one has done it.* Indeed, the bulk of the modifications and revisions to the rules for box girder construction has persuaded many engineers to question seriously the feasibility of using box girders in situations where straightforward plate girders would do equally well.

One is reminded in this example that bridge building is not just the mechanical application of an impersonal technology, but an activity that involves effective human thinking and communication. It is becoming increasingly clear that in building bridges as in most great challenges which face the world today, the limiting factors are not technological, nor even economic, but the human ability to decide on priorities and objectives and to co-operate in getting the job done. The more advanced the technology, the greater the economic pressures, the more crucial become the consequences of human action.

Index

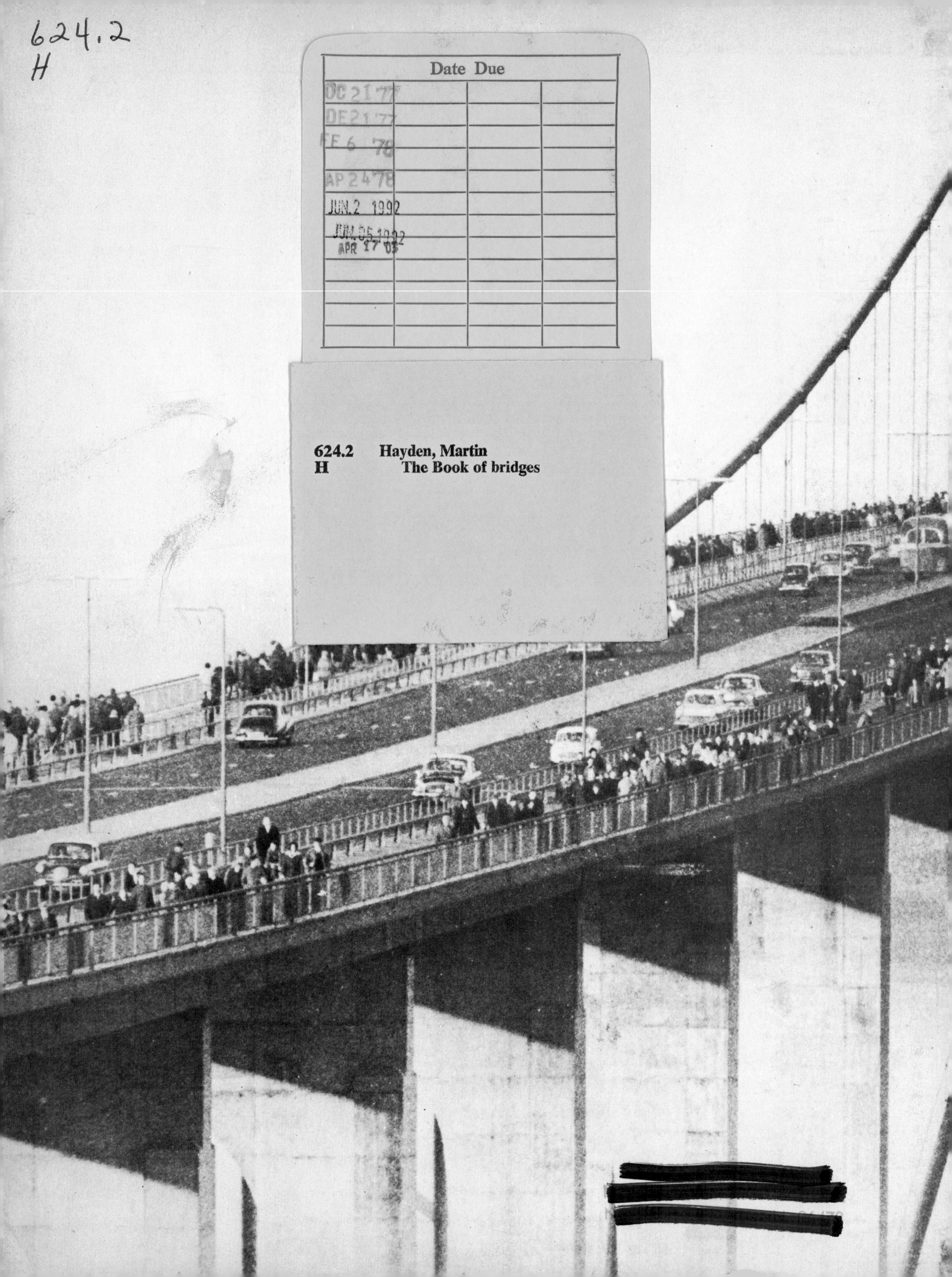